ARROYO CENTER

T0303211

Assessing Security Cooperation as a Preventive Tool

Michael J. McNerney, Angela O'Mahony, Thomas S. Szayna,
Derek Eaton, Caroline Baxter, Colin P. Clarke, Emma Cutrufello,
Michael McGee, Heather Peterson, Leslie Adrienne Payne,
Calin Trenkov-Wermuth

Prepared for the United States Army
Approved for public release; distribution unlimited

The research described in this report was sponsored by the United States Army under Contract No. W74V8H-06-C-0001.

Library of Congress Cataloging-in-Publication Data

McNerney, Michael J.
  Assessing security cooperation as a preventive tool / Michael J. McNerney, Angela O'Mahony, Thomas S. Szayna, Derek Eaton, Caroline Baxter, Colin P. Clarke, Emma Cutrufello, Michael McGee, Heather Peterson, Leslie Adrienne Payne, Calin Trenkov-Wermuth.
      pages cm
  Includes bibliographical references.
  ISBN 978-0-8330-8146-9 (pbk. : alk. paper)
    1. Military assistance, American—Evaluation. 2. Security sector—International cooperation. 3. Conflict management—International cooperation. 4. Terrorism—United States—Prevention. 5. Political stability. 6. Security, International. 7. United States—Military relations. I. Title
  UA23.M254 2014
  355'.031—dc23   2014005202

The RAND Corporation is a nonprofit institution that helps improve policy and decisionmaking through research and analysis. RAND's publications do not necessarily reflect the opinions of its research clients and sponsors.

Support RAND—make a tax-deductible charitable contribution at www.rand.org/giving/contribute.html

RAND® is a registered trademark

RAND OFFICES
SANTA MONICA, CA • WASHINGTON, DC
PITTSBURGH, PA • NEW ORLEANS, LA • JACKSON, MS • BOSTON, MA
DOHA, QA • CAMBRIDGE, UK • BRUSSELS, BE
www.rand.org

Preface

This report documents the results of a project entitled "Assessing Security Cooperation as a Preventive Tool." The project aimed to assess the evidence that security cooperation can be employed to prevent the onset of unrest and instability or other adverse conditions—potentially leading to the development of terrorist safe havens—from occurring in partner states. The analysis was conducted to support the Army leadership on decisions regarding the use of Army's security cooperation.

The report should be of interest to those concerned with the U.S.—and especially the U.S. armed forces—role in global counter-terrorist efforts and actions to reduce unrest and instability in partner states. Research for this project was conducted September 2011–August 2012.

This research was sponsored by the Army Quadrennial Defense Review Office in the Office of the Deputy Chief of Staff, G-8, Headquarters, Department of the Army. The research was conducted within RAND Arroyo Center's Strategy and Resources Program. RAND Arroyo Center, part of the RAND Corporation, is a federally funded research and development center sponsored by the United States Army.

The Project Unique Identification Code for the project that produced this document is HQD116191.

For comments or further information, please contact the project leaders, Michael McNerney (telephone 703-413-1100, extension 5515, email Michael_McNerney@rand.org) and Thomas Szayna (telephone 310-393-0411, extension 7758, email Thomas_Szayna@rand.org).

For more information on RAND Arroyo Center, contact the Director of Operations (telephone 310-393-0411, extension 6419; fax

310-451-6952; email Marcy_Agmon@rand.org) or visit Arroyo's web site at http://www.rand.org/ard.html.

Contents

Figures

Tables

Summary

The Policy Question

Since 2005, U.S. Department of Defense (DoD) policy documents have asserted that security cooperation (SC) can be used to help prevent instability and reduce fragility in partner states. This premise—the preventive hypothesis—has become an important aspect of U.S. global strategy and a strategic pillar for the U.S. Army. The premise has been accepted as intuitively true and backed up by important case studies and numerous anecdotes. Our research had the purpose of assessing empirical support for the preventive hypothesis.

Because the preventive hypothesis underpins U.S. policy goals and applies across all security sectors, we use a modified definition of SC as "activities undertaken by the U.S. government to encourage and enable international partners to work with the United States to achieve security sector objectives."

Using the information provided in policy documents, we explicitly specified the preventive hypothesis. Then, based on the empirical linkage between states' high fragility levels and the incidence of major unrest or instability, we focused on the correlation between SC and reduction in state fragility. We compiled data on SC based on the U.S. Agency for International Development's Greenbook,[1] which captures most foreign assistance (including SC) expenditures, as well as the For-

---

[1] U.S. Agency for International Development, *U.S. Overseas Loans and Grants, Obligations and Loan Authorizations, July 1, 1945–September 30, 2011*, Washington, D.C., 2012, known popularly as the USAID Greenbook.

eign Military Training Report, Government Accountability Office and DoD reports to Congress, and data from DoD's regional centers. We included only concessional aid (e.g., grants), not sales of equipment or services. To assess changes in state fragility, we used the State Fragility Index developed by the Center for Systemic Peace and widely used in the conflict and development communities.

We developed country-year observations using 107 countries from 1991 to 2008, ending up with almost 1,300 observations. While most SC is based on multiple U.S. interests, such as improved access and influence, we excluded only countries where SC was least likely to be motivated by prevention of instability. We normalized expenditures across countries by using SC per capita and by logging the data. We also used standard statistical methods to control for the diversity of countries and other factors that would affect fragility over time independent of SC. Finally, because SC does not produce instant results, we assessed its correlation with partner fragility five years after SC was provided. We also conducted case studies of a dozen countries to gain a more nuanced and rich understanding of the impact of SC in these countries.

Findings

Our findings support the preventive hypothesis. We found that on average SC has a statistically significant relationship with reduction in fragility. The one-year effect is small, with most of the impact concentrated at the low end of expenditures per country, and there are diminishing returns from increased expenditures. It is possible that SC over time could have more significant results. We also found that the correlation of SC with reduction in fragility is nuanced and depends on conditions in the recipient country:

- SC was more highly correlated with reduction in fragility in states with stronger state institutions and greater state reach.
- SC was not correlated with reduction in fragility in states that were already experiencing extremely high fragility.

- SC was more highly correlated with reduction in fragility in more-democratic regimes; the more democratic the regime, the greater the correlation of SC and reduction in fragility.
- The concentration of low state reach, authoritarian regimes, and relatively high levels of fragility in the Middle East and Africa meant that the positive correlation of SC and reduction in fragility was least pronounced in those regions; Latin America, Asia Pacific, and Europe had the best effects.

Some types of U.S. SC are more highly correlated with reductions in state fragility than others. Nonmateriel aid, such as education, law enforcement, and counternarcotics aid, were more highly correlated; provision of materiel aid, even though it forms the majority of U.S. SC, was not correlated with reducing fragility in recipient countries. This outcome may stem from the fact that materiel aid is often focused on goals other than reducing state fragility, such as strengthening relationships, improving U.S. military access to a country, and improving capabilities for external defense.

We did not find development aid from the United States or other developed countries to have a statistically significant effect on the effectiveness of U.S. SC. That may be due to the fact that much development assistance goes to the most fragile states and, based on recent trends in understanding the effect of development aid, because development aid appears to work on longer time frames than security aid.

Implications

Our research has established a statistically significant correlation between U.S. SC spending and improvement in the recipient country's fragility, but many unknowns remain concerning the preventive hypothesis. The effect was weakest in countries with high fragility scores and thus most at risk of state failure, and greatest in those where instability and state failure are highly unlikely. This suggests that SC may be better at "reinforcing success" or preventing backsliding than in halting a country's decline into instability.

Education offers the greatest impact in terms of categories of SC in reducing fragility. This finding supports the general idea that investment in human capital has large payoffs. But education is also the smallest of the categories we examined. There may be a ceiling as to how effective such programs might be if these programs were to be expanded. The finding that law enforcement and counternarcotics programs appear to have better results than traditional train and equip efforts needs to be examined more closely to determine whether their success stems from being well integrated into broader whole of government efforts.

Our findings suggest that, in situations of high fragility, SC is not sufficient to stave off instability, because highly fragile partner states are not able to use SC effectively. This point highlights the importance of prevention. In such cases, as well as in cases of partners lacking state reach, a more-coordinated aid program of development and security aid and a focus on institution building may be a better approach. In some cases of low state reach, development assistance, with its long-term focus, may be a better tool than SC.

The high correlation of small amounts of SC with a reduction in fragility and the fact that returns diminish rapidly with increased investments points to intriguing insights, such as the possibility that it is the fact of U.S. involvement itself—with its diplomatic and political backing—rather than its form or size that had the greatest impact on state fragility.

With judgment, the results of our study can be used for decision-making concerning the type of SC to provide on the basis of state characteristics. Our findings may provide better grounds for expectation management when it comes to provision of SC to highly fragile states. Our findings also may be of interest to SC planners at geographic combatant commands.

Our results suggest that training and education efforts make a real contribution to reducing fragility and preventing conflict. The Army's increased focus on SC, as shown by designating brigades for SC and aligning these units along regional lines, is a step that is in accordance with greater U.S. conflict-prevention efforts. Increased emphasis on low-footprint special operations forces efforts to build partner capacity is also in line with the preventive hypothesis that is supported by our study.

Acknowledgments

The authors are grateful to LTG Robert P. Lennox, HQDA G-8, for sponsoring the study. We thank Timothy Muchmore, HQDA G-8, for monitoring the study and providing constructive feedback during its course. At G-8, we also would like to thank Volney (Jim) Warner and Joseph McInnis for their support and interest in the study.

Many people at the Joint Staff, Office of the Secretary of Defense for Policy, and HQDA G-3 provided comments in the course of the study. We thank them for their time and interest.

At RAND, we are indebted to Chris Paul, Beth Grill, Adam Grissom, Frank Camm, Paul Heaton, Jennifer Moroney, and Stephen Watts for helping out with data and for providing comments in the course of the study. MAJ Kirk Windmueller participated in the project and helped shape the thinking of the project staff.

Keith Crane, Agnes Schaefer, and Patrick Cronin provided formal reviews of the draft report of this study. Jerry Sollinger improved the structure of the document. Julie Ann Tajiri and Rosa Meza formatted the draft. Nikki Shacklett edited the report and formatted the final version.

A large team of analysts contributed to this effort. Michael McNerney, Angela O'Mahony, and Thomas Szayna are the lead authors of this report. Their names appear in alphabetical order.

Abbreviations

ADP	Army Doctrine Publication
AECA	Arms Export Control Act
AFRICOM	U.S. Africa Command
AIDS	Acquired Immune Deficiency Syndrome.
BPC	Building Partner Capacity
CN	counternarcotics
CSP	Center for Systemic Peace
CT	counterterrorism
DAMI-CDS	Deputy Chief of Staff for Intelligence/Counterintelligence, Human Intelligence, Security and Disclosure
DAMI-FL	Deputy Chief of Staff for Intelligence/Foreign Liaison
DAMO-SSI	Strategy, Plans and Policy Directorate/Multinational Strategy and Programs
DAMO-SSO	Strategy, Plans and Policy Directorate/Stability Operations
DAMO-SSR	Strategy, Plans and Policy Directorate/Strategic Planning, Concepts and Doctrine
DoD	Department of Defense
DoS	Department of State
EUCOM	U.S. European Command

FID	foreign internal defense
FM	field manual
FMF	Foreign Military Finance
FMFP	Foreign Military Financing Program
FMS	foreign military sales
FMTR	Foreign Military Training Reports
GCC	geographic combatant command
GDP	gross domestic product
GPOI	Global Peace Operations Initiative
HQDA	Headquarters, Department of the Army
HQDA G-2	Deputy Chief of Staff for Intelligence
HQDA G-3	Deputy Chief of Staff for Operations
HQDA G-3/5/7	Deputy Chief of Staff for Operations and Plans
HQDA G-8	Deputy Chief of Staff for Programs
HQDA G-35	Deputy Chief of Staff for Operations and Plans
IMET	International Military Education and Training
INCLE	International Narcotics Control and Law Enforcement
JOC	Joint Operating Concept
MAP	Military Assistance Program
MEDCOM	U.S. Army Medical Command
MEPV	Major Episodes of Political Violence
NATO	North Atlantic Treaty Organization
NDAA	National Defense Authorization Act
NGB	National Guard Bureau
NMS	National Military Strategy
NSDD	National Security Decision Directive
NSS	National Security Strategy
OECD	Organization for Economic Cooperation and Development

PACOM	U.S. Pacific Command
PEPFAR	President's Emergency Plan for AIDS Relief
QDR	Quadrennial Defense Review
SA	security assistance
SATFA	Security Assistance Training Field Activity
SC	security cooperation
SFA	security force assistance
SFI	State Fragility Index
SOUTHCOM	U.S. Southern Command
SPP	State Partnership Program
TRADOC	U.S. Army Training and Doctrine Command
USAID	U.S. Agency for International Development
USMA	U.S. Military Academy
WMD	weapons of mass destruction

CHAPTER ONE

Introduction

The Context

In 2005 the Department of Defense (DoD) moved to embrace the idea that the United States can employ security cooperation (SC) to help prevent the development of terrorist sanctuaries or other adverse conditions in partner states. According to this idea (from here on referred to as "the preventive hypothesis"), SC missions are cost-beneficial to attempt even where the prospects for "success" are low—either because there is uncertainty about the true seriousness of the threat to the partner state or because the probability of direct U.S. involvement in the partner state appears minimal—because they can be conducted for a small fraction of the cost of direct U.S. involvement. The 2006 *Quadrennial Defense Review*[1] (QDR) made the preventive hypothesis a key part of U.S. national security policy. Since then, the preventive hypothesis has been codified in numerous DoD policy documents, including the military and defense strategies and internal DoD guidance documents.[2]

The initial focus on preventive SC as part of a counterterrorist strategy remains in place, although the same conditions of state fragility and weakness that DoD policy posits as being conducive to establishment of terrorist safe havens also apply to international drug

---

[1] DoD, *Quadrennial Defense Review Report*, February 6, 2006a.

[2] The idea of using U.S. SC as a tool to prevent emergence of conflict may have been implicit prior to 2005, but the concept became explicit and formalized in policy documents beginning in 2005.

traffickers and other transnational criminal organizations. In a wider sense, state weakness and fragility can lead to conflicts that cross borders and destabilize entire regions; cause humanitarian crises; and threaten international development, trade, and energy supplies. This wider focus is clear in the 2010 QDR, which states that building the capacity of partners to maintain and promote stability helps prevent conflict and other threats to U.S. interests.[3]

Since the initial policy guidance, DoD has moved to increase resources and capabilities for SC by, among other things, greatly expanding special forces; enlarging the elements in the U.S. Air Force, Navy, and Marine Corps dedicated to SC; and creating the new "1200 series" authorities and funding sources for SC.[4] The Army, building on its extensive experience with SFA in Iraq and Afghanistan, is developing plans to use Army general purpose forces for SC. Especially in planning for the post-2014 security environment, the preventive thesis is a central strategic pillar for the U.S. Army and conceptually links SC programs, which build the capacity of partners, with reduced state fragility and U.S. interests.

Although the preventive hypothesis is now an important assumption for U.S. defense policy, data in support of the hypothesis have not been examined thoroughly, and the logic underlying it remains underspecified. For instance, various DoD sources offer different interpretations, many of which are not fully described in terms of causal linkages, essential assumptions, and necessary conditions. Moreover, there is a lack of detailed empirical research into the question of whether there is real evidence that SC has successfully been employed as a preventive mechanism. If DoD is going to continue to shift resources toward SC, there is a need to ascertain if and to what extent SC can be used to advance U.S. security goals by decreasing state fragility in partner states.

---

[3] DoD, *Quadrennial Defense Review Report*, February 2010, p. 13.

[4] This includes the 1206 (counterterrorism), 1207 (stabilization assistance), and 1208 (special operations forces assistance in counterterrorism) programs. We discuss these in more detail in Chapter Three.

Terminology

Before proceeding further, we define some key terms. Because the preventive hypothesis underpins U.S. policy goals and applies across the defense and law enforcement components of the security sector, we define SC as "activities undertaken by the U.S. government to encourage and enable international partners to work with the United States to achieve security sector objectives." This is a modification of a definition set down in DoD doctrine in 2008, with the differences being that we use the term "U.S. government" rather than "Department of Defense" and replace "strategic" with "security sector."[5] SC thus covers a broad range of DoD, Department of State (DoS), and other activities from individual interactions, to unit exercises, to large train and equip programs.

SC encompasses and overlaps three other capacity-building oriented concepts: security assistance (SA), foreign internal defense (FID), and security force assistance (SFA). Generally, in terms of dollars spent, SA is the largest component of SC. SA is not a specific activity; rather it is a group of programs authorized by the Foreign Assistance Act of 1961, the Arms Export Control Act of 1976, and other related statutes through which the United States provides defense articles, military training, and other defense-related services by grant, loan, credit, or cash sales in support of U.S. national interests. SA programs are funded and authorized by the DoS but are primarily administered by DoD.[6] DoD describes FID as the

> participation by civilian and military agencies of a government in any of the action programs taken by another government or other designated organization to free and protect its society from subversion, lawlessness, insurgency, terrorism, and other threats to its security.[7]

---

[5]   Department of Defense Directive 5132.03, "DoD Policy and Responsibilities Relating to Security Cooperation," October 24, 2008.

[6]   Joint Publication 1-02, *Department of Defense Dictionary of Military and Associated Terms*," August 2012, p. 275.

[7]   JP 1-02, 2012, p. 121.

FID encompasses both combat and noncombat operations and seeks to increase the military, governmental, societal, and economic capacity of a state through both security and economic assistance. SC and SA provide some of the tools used to conduct FID. SFA is a collection of DoD activities that contribute to unified action by the U.S. government to support the development of the capacity and capability of foreign security forces and their supporting institutions.[8] SFA is focused on capacity building in response to both external and internal threats and is enabled by funds provided through SA and similar DoD programs, such as the Building Partner Capacity of Foreign Militaries program (section 1206).[9] Figure 1.1 shows the Army's description of the complex relationship between these four concepts, as explained in doctrine.

To capture the largest SC activities for our analysis, we focus primarily on programs that assist foreign security forces and that are identified in the U.S. Agency for International Development's (USAID's) "U.S. Overseas Loans and Grants" annual report to Congress and the Foreign Military Training Reports (FMTR) issued by DoD and the DoS.[10] Not all SC programs are included in our analysis, e.g., military service–managed SC (we include Army programs in Appendix B for completeness and context). We discuss this further in our discussion of methodology in Chapter Three.

Objectives and Organization

The Army, along with other services, has used SC programs to work with other militaries for decades in pursuit of a variety of goals, as outlined by DoD (build defense relationships, develop capabilities of partners for self-defense and coalition operations, improve U.S. mili-

---

[8] JP 1-02, 2012, p. 276.

[9] SFA is also enabled by country-specific funding, such as the Afghanistan Security Forces Fund and the Iraq Security Forces Fund.

[10] USAID, *U.S. Overseas Loans and Grants: Obligations and Loan Authorizations, July 1, 1945–September 30, 2011*, Washington, D.C., 2012 (also known as the Greenbook); Department of Defense and Department of State, *Foreign Military Training*, Vol. 1, joint report to Congress, fiscal years 1999–2011.

Figure 1.1
U.S. Army Description of the Relationship Between Security Cooperation, Security Assistance, Foreign Internal Defense, and Security Force Assistance

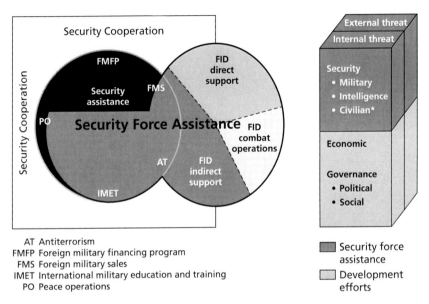

AT Antiterrorism
FMFP Foreign military financing program
FMS Foreign military sales
IMET International military education and training
PO Peace operations

Security force assistance
Development efforts

*U.S. Army forces only assist in establishing civil control with Congressional approval.
SOURCE: Army Field Manual (FM) 3-07.1, "Security Force Assistance," Washington, D.C.: Headquarters, Department of the Army, May 2009, pp. 1–7.
NOTE: Our definition of Security Cooperation includes law enforcement, counternarcotics, and other activities undertaken by the DoS and other non-DoD agencies.
RAND *RR350-1.1*

tary access). As the main provider of U.S. land power and the service that provides the majority of U.S. SC, the Army seeks to improve its understanding of the value of SC to help prevent instability. Such an understanding is critical for effective resource allocations for SC and for the development of Army units most effective at providing SC. Consequently, the Army asked RAND Arroyo Center for analytical assistance. Specifically, the project had the following objectives:

- Fully specify the preventive hypothesis and then derive testable subhypotheses for the study.

- Assess the empirical validity of the preventive hypothesis, relying on the best available U.S. government data and scholarly literature and databases.
- Identify key insights and implications for the Army, with particular emphasis on effective use of SC.

This report presents the results of our analysis.

Chapter Two outlines the preventive thesis and the conceptual links among SC, stability, state fragility, and U.S. interests. We relied on policy documents and direct knowledge of policy debates in the DoD in 2005–2010 to inform our thinking.

Chapter Three describes the methodology we used in our statistical analysis of the preventive hypothesis. We compared the extent of U.S. SC effort with changes in state fragility over a 20-year period. We used U.S. government data on expenditures on SC programs to measure the U.S. level of SC effort. We used an academic dataset, the State Fragility Index, to assess a country's fragility. Using standard statistical techniques, we then tested the preventive hypothesis, limiting our analysis to the states where the preventive thesis is applicable.

Chapter Four outlines the findings from our statistical analysis of the preventive hypothesis. We provide findings of the main hypothesis and its several corollaries.

Chapter Five summarizes the findings of the case study analyses that we conducted to gain a more in-depth understanding of the country-specific circumstances that led to changes in state fragility and the role that U.S. SC may have played in those changes.

Chapter Six presents our overall findings and outlines some of the implications of our study for DoD and Army planning of SC for preventive purposes.

Several appendixes provide supporting material and additional information relevant to our study. Appendix A contains an overview of Army SC programs not included in our statistical analysis (since our focus is on an overall U.S. level of effort, our statistical analysis takes into account all the major DoD programs but not necessarily the smaller service programs). Appendix B describes the sensitivity analyses we conducted as part of our research.

The bulk of research and statistical analysis for this project took place between October 2011 and May 2012. We conducted further analyses and case studies until July 2012. From May to September 2012, project team members presented the findings contained in this report to Army and DoD audiences. The draft report was completed in October 2012. It was formally reviewed in February and March 2013. The report was revised in April 2013.

CHAPTER TWO

Security Cooperation, U.S. Strategy, and the Concept of "Prevention"

Since 2005, U.S. strategy documents have taken as a given that SC to bolster a partner state's security institutions can be used as a preventive measure to reduce fragility and decrease the need for larger and more-extensive U.S. military interventions. The belief in the preventive benefits of SC and SFA is also reflected in U.S. Army doctrine.

Because the concept of "prevention" has been developed over six years, across two administrations, and by many organizations, the terminology used to articulate it can be inconsistent and confusing. This chapter provides an overview of the key U.S. security policy documents that outline the preventive hypothesis. The chapter relies on policy documents and on the insights of one of the authors of this report (McNerney), who worked in the DoD during the time frame examined and participated in the policy deliberations. The chapter then notes the relevant U.S. Army documents that internalize the preventive hypothesis, and finally presents our summary of the preventive hypothesis. We close the chapter with a summary of our review of the literature directly relevant to the preventive hypothesis.

National Security Documents

The concept of "preventive action" appeared as an important element of the U.S. strategic lexicon during the drafting of the 2006 QDR. The QDR posited that, as part of its transformation, DoD needed to address the challenges of the "new strategic environment" and that it was necessary to shift the military from a reactive posture to a pro-active one. The 2006 QDR stated that early preventive measures to strengthen fragile states could stop problems from becoming conflicts or crises. The QDR put forth the concept that increasing the capacity of partner states to govern, administer, provide security, and observe the rule of law to improve the legitimacy of these states in the eyes of their people was a way to "inoculate societies against terrorism, insurgency, and non-state threats" and thus prevent terrorist attacks on the United States by denying the terrorists sanctuary and separating them from host populations.[1] The subsequent Building Partner Capacity (BPC) QDR Execution roadmap clarified further the counterterror focus and prophylactic nature of BPC as a preventive action.[2] It stated that the United States will need to work to build the capacities of new international partners "to reduce the drivers of instability, prevent terrorist attacks or disrupt their networks, to deny sanctuary to terrorists anywhere in the world, to separate terrorists from host populations and ultimately to defeat them."[3] The BPC roadmap also noted that "security cooperation activities are aimed at preventing future crises" and, should that effort fail, ensuring that U.S. partners could respond as necessary.[4]

The 2008 DoD's *Military Contribution to Cooperative Security (CS) Joint Operating Concept* (JOC) shed further light on the idea of SC as a preventive tool.[5] It stated that cooperative security efforts focus on maintaining and enhancing stability, preventing and mitigating crises, and enabling operations should these efforts fail.[6] The JOC's pri-

---

[1]   DoD, 2006a, pp. vi, 2–3, 17, 88–90.

[2]   DoD, "QDR Execution Roadmap: Building Partnership Capacity," May 22, 2006b.

[3]   DoD, 2006b, pp. 5–6.

[4]   DoD, 2006b, p. 14.

[5]   DoD, *Military Contribution to Cooperative Security (CS) Joint Operating Concept*, Version 1.0, September 19, 2008.

[6]   Cooperative security is defined as a "set of continuous, long-term integrated comprehensive actions among a broad spectrum of U.S. and international governmental and nongovernmental partners that maintains or enhances stability, prevents or mitigates crisis, and enables operations when crises occur." See DoD 2008, pp. iii, B-4.

mary focus was on steady-state activities "undertaken well in advance of any crisis precipitating event," and it assumed that early engagement could mitigate many problems.[7] It posited that future adversaries will seek to exploit instability to undermine partnerships and further destabilize weak governments; deny or disrupt U.S. influence or access; and gain sanctuary in ungoverned, unstable, and remote areas.[8] According to the JOC, some of the ways that building partner capacity or SC could address these problems was by increasing partner capacity to meet internal and external threats and by enhancing a partner's ability to govern and manage its security institutions.[9] Among the overarching objectives of cooperative security are "thwarting the emergence of security threats and contributing to initiatives that alleviate the underlying conditions, motivators, and enablers of violent extremism and destabilizing militancy."[10] According to the JOC, successful cooperative security would result in improved security, nonproliferation, political stability, good governance, sustained development, legitimate competition and trade, and economic prosperity.[11] The JOC posited that, in support of the U.S. counterterrorism strategy, the primary objective of cooperative security is to help alleviate the underlying conditions, motivators, and enablers of violent extremism. In the JOC's perspective, the influence of such violently inclined groups over a local population can be reduced by creating favorable political, social, and economic outcomes.[12]

Then Secretary of Defense Robert Gates provided greater clarity to the concepts outlined above in a *Foreign Affairs* article in early 2009. He argued that it was necessary to build host nation government and security force capacity to prevent "festering problems" from turning into crises that required "costly and controversial direct military

---

[7] DoD, 2008, pp. iii, 2, 8.

[8] DoD, 2008, p. 5.

[9] DoD, 2008, pp. 19–20.

[10] DoD, 2008, p. 10.

[11] DoD, 2008, p. 8.

[12] DoD, 2008, pp. 31–32.

action."[13] He warned that failing states and insurgencies were danger-
ous because terrorists could use weak states as sanctuaries and gain
strength from internal disorder. The problem could become particularly acute if the failing state also had nuclear weapons. Secretary Gates
asserted that, due to this posited nexus of failed states, nuclear weapons, and terrorism, the most likely catastrophic threats to the United
States would emanate from these failed states rather than aggressor
states.[14] Consequently, dealing with weak states represented a key U.S.
security challenge, a challenge best met by building partner capacity.[15]

The key strategic documents produced by President Obama's
administration—the 2010 *National Security Strategy* (NSS), the 2011
National Military Strategy (NMS), and the 2010 QDR—largely incor-
porated the strategic concerns and ideas outlined above.[16] Indeed, the
2010 NSS argues strongly for early preventive action and justifies it
because

> proactively investing in stronger societies and human welfare is
> far more effective than responding after state collapse. The United
> States must improve its capability to strengthen the security of
> states at risk of conflict and violence.[17]

The NSS outlines that the United States will "undertake long-term
sustained efforts to strengthen the capacity of security forces to guar-
antee internal security, defend against internal threats, and promote
regional security and respect human rights and the rule of law."[18] The

---

[13] Robert M. Gates, "A Balanced Strategy: Reprogramming the Pentagon for a New Age,"
Foreign Affairs, Vol. 88, No. 1, January/February 2009, pp. 29–30. See also Robert M.
Gates, "Helping Others Defend Themselves: The Future of U.S. Security Assistance," *For-
eign Affairs*, Vol. 89, No. 3, May/June 2010, pp. 2–6.

[14] Gates, 2009, pp. 29–30.

[15] Gates, 2010, pp. 2–6.

[16] White House, *National Security Strategy*, Washington, D.C., May 2010; DoD, *The
National Military Strategy of the United States of America 2011: Redefining America's Military
Leadership*, February 2011; and DoD, *Quadrennial Defense Review Report*, February 2010.

[17] White House, 2010, p. 27.

[18] White House, 2010, p. 27.

NSS justifies the requirement on the basis of the belief that the internal collapse of a state can present a security threat to the U.S. population, the U.S. homeland, and to U.S. interests, particularly if it enables violent extremists to acquire nuclear weapons.[19] More specifically, such activity is important because denying safe havens and strengthening at-risk states is a component of the U.S. strategy to defeat al-Qa'ida. Accomplishing the strategy entails helping states "avoid becoming terrorist safe havens by helping them build their capacity for responsible governance and security through development and security force assistance."[20] Finally, the NSS posits that it is the underlying political and economic weaknesses that foster instability, enable radicalization and extremism, and undermine the ability of a government to manage threats within their borders. The consequences of a foreign government's failure to meet its citizens' basic needs and to provide security are "often global and may directly threaten the American people."[21] The 2010 NSS also adds preventing "genocide and mass atrocities" as a national goal.

The 2010 QDR expands on and makes more explicit the nascent "prevent" concepts put forward by the 2006 QDR. It states that it "brings fresh focus to the importance of preventing and deterring conflict by working with and through allies and partners" and that building partner capacity to maintain and promote stability is necessary to prevent the rise of threats to U.S. interests.[22] According to the 2010 QDR, strengthening weak states is important because conflict is as likely to arise from state weakness as from state strength and because chronically fragile states are "often catalysts for the growth of radicalism and extremism." The failure of a nuclear state is particularly threatening to U.S. interests.[23] From such a perspective, building partner capacity becomes important in preventing conflicts from beginning

---

[19] White House, 2010, pp. 4, 17.

[20] White House, 2010, p. 21.

[21] White House, 2010, p. 26.

[22] DoD, 2010, pp. i, v.

[23] DoD, 2010, pp. 9, 28.

or escalating and in reducing the possibility that large and enduring deployments of U.S. forces will be required. Building partner security capacity can also reduce the scope and scale of al-Qa'ida safe havens and prevent their reconstitution.[24] This last result is important because, according to the QDR, terrorists exploit ungoverned or undergoverned territory and use it to recruit, train, and plan attacks against the United States. The phenomenon can be prevented by professional security forces that protect local populations from terrorist and insurgent threats.[25]

The final strategic document relevant to our research is the 2011 NMS. Since it is based on the NSS and the QDR, the NMS, to a large extent, reiterates the ideas articulated in the other two documents. As such, it notes that "states with weak, failing, and corrupt governments increasingly will be used as safe havens for an expanding array of non-state actors that breed conflict and endanger stability" and that there is a need to prevent tensions from escalating into conflict.[26] The NMS claims that BPC can help prevent such problems because it helps reduce potential safe havens before "violent extremism can take root" and that it is necessary to focus these efforts on critical states "where the threat of terrorism could pose a threat to [U.S.] homeland and interests."[27] Finally, the NMS notes in the context of deterrence that "preventing wars is as important as winning them, and far less costly."[28]

Army Doctrine

Current Army doctrine supports the idea that increasing partner capacity can be used as a preventive tool. However, it has very little to say on the causal links between SC and SFA and the prevention of nega-

---

[24] DoD, 2010, pp. 10–11, 27, 28, 44.

[25] DoD, 2010, p. 27.

[26] DoD, 2011, pp. 4–5.

[27] DoD, 2011, pp. 6, 12.

[28] DoD, 2011, p. 7.

tive internal outcomes. One of the Army's main doctrinal documents, Army Doctrine Publication (ADP) 3-0, recognizes that Build Partner Capacity is an important Army mission,[29] and it notes that BPC results in a partner's enhanced ability to provide "security, governance, economic development, essential services, rule of law, and other critical government functions."[30] ADP 3-0 does not contain a discussion of the preventive BPC concept beyond the assumption that all Army actions can be used to prevent or deter conflicts and create conditions for favorable conflict resolution.

Aspects of the Army's doctrine on stability operations have an important preventive quality. FM 3-07 states in its preface that

> this manual also provides doctrine on how those capabilities are leveraged to support a partner nation as part of peacetime military engagement. Those activities, executed in a relatively benign security environment as an element of a combatant commander's theater security cooperation plans, share many of the same broad goals as stability operations conducted after a conflict or disaster. Such activities aim to build partner capacity, strengthen legitimate governance, maintain rule of law, foster economic growth, and help to forge a strong sense of national unity. Ideally, these are addressed before, rather than after, conflict. Conducted within the context of peacetime military engagement, they are essential to sustaining the long-term viability of host nations and provide the foundation for multinational cooperation that helps to maintain the global balance of power.[31]

FM 3-07 largely mirrors the language of the QDR and other strategic documents by noting that stability operations can reduce the drivers of instability (religious fanaticism, global competition for resources,

---

[29] The Army's terminology differs a bit from DoD's, with the Army using the term Build Partner Capacity.

[30] Army Doctrine Publication 3-0, "Unified Land Operations," Washington, D.C.: Headquarters, Department of the Army, October 2011, p. 3.

[31] Army Field Manual 3-07, "Stability Operations," Washington, D.C.: Headquarters, Department of the Army, October 2008, p. vii.

climate change, territorial claims, ideology, ethnic tension, greed, and the desire for power) and build host nation capacity that will result in a sustainable peace, security, and economic growth. Included in this concept is security sector reform, a concept similar to SFA.[32] The goal of a stability operation is "conflict transformation." Conflict transformation changes the nature of the competition by reducing the motivations for violent action while developing more peaceful competitive alternatives. It does this by identifying the root causes of conflict and instability and developing an integrated strategy for resolving them by building a local capacity for effective governance, economic development, and the rule of law.[33]

Borrowing from USAID work on fragile states, FM 3-07 identifies "fragile states as being of particular concern." It defines a fragile state as a "country that suffers from institutional weaknesses serious enough to threaten the stability of the central government." Such weakness can emerge from a variety of causes, including ineffective governance, criminalization of the state, economic failure, external aggression, and internal unrest resulting from the denial of political rights to large segments of the state's population. Such problems have the potential to result in large-scale human suffering, regional instability, and the creation of ungoverned spaces that can be exploited by terrorist and criminal groups. [34] FM 3-07 notes that fragile states can be classified further as being either vulnerable or crisis states. A *vulnerable state* is one that cannot provide adequate security or essential services to a large section of its population. As a result, the legitimacy of its central government is at risk. A *crisis state* is one where the central government does not have effective control over its territory. Crisis states include failing or failed states and are either engulfed by or at significant risk of violent conflict.[35]

---

[32] FM 3-07, 2008, pp. 1-2 to 1-3.

[33] FM 3-07, 2008, p. 1-6.

[34] FM 3-07, 2008, p. 1-10.

[35] FM 3-07, 2008, p. 1-10.

Borrowing from the then-current (2006) NSS, FM 3-07 notes that stability tasks conducted as part of a theater SC plan can foster democracy and economic development and thus prevent the emergence of conflicts."[36] FM 3-07 also notes that security is "essential for legitimate governance and participation, effective rule of law, and sustained economic development" and that "an effective security sector fosters development, encourages foreign investments, and helps reduce poverty." It also states that establishing security in a country requires the elimination of the drivers of conflict. Such an end is enabled by a security establishment that is transparent, accountable to the civilian government, and responsive to the needs of the public.[37] Finally, FM 3-07 highlights the importance of a competent, law-abiding, and civilian-controlled military for government legitimacy and national stability.

SFA, a key component of the stability operation tasks of establishing civil security and civil authority, focuses on improving the capacity of a host nation's security forces and is generally, but not exclusively, conducted as a component of stability operations.[38] FM 3-07.1 focuses primarily on the nuts and bolts of providing SFA through the deployment of brigade combat teams and on how soldiers can advise foreign security forces.[39] It does note, however, that SFA can be a component of a host state's internal defense and development plan, which focuses on building viable institutions that respond to societal needs. The plan can be preventive in that it "aims to forestall or defeat the threat and to correct core grievances that prompt violence. Ideally it is a preemptive strategy."[40] As the above demonstrates, the Army's doctrine has integrated key elements of the national-level preventive hypothesis.

---

[36] FM 3-07, 2008, pp. 1-11 to 1-12.

[37] FM 3-07, 2008, p. 6-1.

[38] FM 3-07.1, 2009, p. 1-1.

[39] FM 3-07.1, 2009, p. iv.

[40] FM 3-07.1, 2009, pp. 1-6 to 1-7.

The Preventive Hypothesis

The preceding discussion indicates that national-level strategic documents accept, and depend on, the idea that the United States can use SC as a tool early enough to help prevent a partner state from weakening to the point that conflict erupts or terrorists can use its territory to threaten the United States. The preventive hypothesis also has become internalized in the U.S. Army's doctrine.

Based on our examination of the U.S. strategy documents, the causal chain supporting the preventive hypothesis starts off with the idea that weak governmental, economic, and security institutions lead to instability that in turn fosters unacceptable levels of violence or insurgency, which threaten U.S. interests (see Figure 2.1). The instability resulting from weak institutions can have several potential negative outcomes for U.S. security, such as

1. It can allow terrorists to establish safe havens or a recruiting base.
2. It can result in the loss of control of a nuclear (or other weapons of mass destruction [WMD]) arsenal with some of the weapons ending up in terrorist hands.
3. It can lead to a costly, lengthy, and unpopular U.S. intervention.

The preventive hypothesis assumes that U.S. SC efforts will lead to stronger host-state institutions (security or otherwise), thereby making a country less fragile and thus better able to resist shocks that

Figure 2.1
The Preventive Hypothesis Causal Chain: Problem Identification

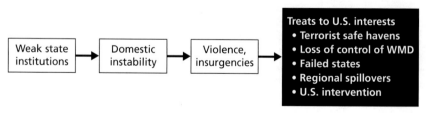

SOURCE: RAND portrayal based on examination of policy documents.
RAND RR350-2.1

foster instability and provide opportunities for hostile actors to exploit to the detriment of U.S. interests (see Figure 2.2). Accepting the above logic, theoretically, strengthening critical institutions early enough can prevent negative outcomes to U.S. security.

The preventive hypothesis makes sense intuitively. However, as we discuss below, our literature review did not turn up empirical evidence to support it. Furthermore, some of the relevant research that we did find is not encouraging, in that SC during the Cold War was associated with an increased probability of military coups, strengthened military regimes, and regional arms races.[41] These findings may be dated, in that bilateral U.S.-Soviet rivalry during the Cold War determined the type and size of SC, sparked a counterreaction, and may have led to the adverse political outcomes. Therefore, we have focused on the post–Cold War era and assessed the effects of SC on a host state's internal stability in the post–Cold War period and explore the validity of the broader preventive hypothesis.

We are not aware of any datasets that would allow us to measure directly the impact of SC on institutional strength and the effect of institutional strength on domestic stability. Instead, as we discuss in Chapter Three, we use a state's "fragility score," as measured by the State Fragility Index, as a proxy for this process.[42] We do this because

Figure 2.2
The Preventive Hypothesis Causal Chain: Security Cooperation as a Preventive Mechanism

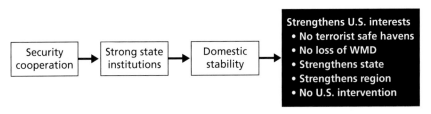

SOURCE: RAND portrayal based on examination of policy documents.
RAND RR350-2.2

---

[41] The first two of these findings were not necessarily detrimental to short- or medium-term U.S. security interests.

[42] We discuss the State Fragility Index in greater depth in Chapter Three.

the preventive hypothesis rests on the idea that improved state institutions make a state stronger and less fragile. The causal mechanism we are thus testing is that SC reduces a state's fragility.

As shown in Table 2.1, more fragile states have a greater probability of undergoing the onset of a period of instability potentially severe enough to trigger a U.S. intervention. The left column of Table 2.1 shows the categories of fragility.[43] Based on historical data from 1996–2009, the middle column shows the probability of instability for states in each category of fragility. The instability measured includes the onset of an ethnic or revolutionary war, genocides or politicides, and adverse regime changes.[44] The right column shows the historically derived average length of years of stability for the states in that category of fragility. The historical data in Table 2.1 indicate that

Table 2.1
Probabilistic Link Between State Fragility and Instability

	Yearly Probability of Instability Onset (%)	Average Years of Stability
Extreme fragility	8.82	11.3
High fragility	5.85	17.1
Serious fragility	2.05	48.8
Moderate fragility	1.35	74.1
Low fragility	1.03	97.1
Little to no fragility	0	—

SOURCE: Monty G. Marshall and Benjamin R. Cole, *Global Report 2009: Conflict, Governance and State Fragility*, Vienna, Va.: Center for Systemic Peace, December 2009a, p. 22.

---

[43] The State Fragility Index has a 26-point scale, 0 being least fragile and 25 being most fragile. The distinctions are as follows: 0–3, Little or No Fragility; 4–7, Low Fragility; 8–11, Moderate Fragility; 12–15, Serious Fragility; 16–19, High Fragility; 20–25, Extreme Fragility.

[44] An adverse regime change is a six-point or more decrease in a state's polity score (i.e., a steep drop in its level of democratization) or the collapse of its central authority (a score of –77).

a high level of state fragility is related to major episodes of instability, with the likelihood of instability rising sharply for High Fragility and Extreme Fragility states.

To reiterate, we used these findings to underpin how we went about testing the preventive hypothesis. We tested whether SC reduces a state's fragility score (that is, increases its resiliency) and consequently lowers the probability that it will undergo a severe instability event. We thus tested whether SC lowers the probability of domestic instability. In addition, we tested several conditional hypotheses to see whether the effects of SC on increasing state resiliency vary by such factors as regime type, region, the receipt of development assistance, or the type of SC provided (foreign military financing, other train and equip, law enforcement and counternarcotics, or education).

Related Research

As we noted above, there is little empirical research on the effect of SC on receiving countries. We did not find any cross-sectional time-series studies that examined the effect of military or security aid on a country's stability and political development. In fact, the literature on military aid has tended to focus on evaluating the effectiveness of individual programs or on the impact of military aid on specific countries (using case study approaches). Recent research on U.S. SC has examined the effectiveness of specific aid programs, such as antiterror aid,[45] building capacity for coalition operations,[46] and counterproliferation.[47] Other analyses of SC assess the goals, policies, and organiza-

---

[45] Navin A. Bapat, "Transnational Terrorism, U.S. Military Aid, and the Incentive to Misrepresent," *Journal of Peace Research*, Vol. 48, No. 3, May 1, 2011, pp. 303–318.

[46] Jennifer D. P. Moroney, Beth Grill, Joe Hogler, Lianne Kennedy-Boudali, and Christopher Paul, *How Successful Are U.S. Efforts to Build Capacity in Developing Countries? A Framework to Assess the Global Train and Equip "1206" Program*, Santa Monica, Calif.: RAND Corporation, TR-1121-OSD, 2011.

[47] Moroney, Jennifer D. P., Aidan Kirby Winn, Jeffrey Engstrom, Joe Hogler, Thomas-Durell Young, and Michelle Spencer, *Assessing the Effectiveness of the International Counterproliferation Program*, Santa Monica, Calif.: RAND Corporation, TR-981-DTRA, 2011.

tions making up SC and point to areas for improving how the United States evaluates SC.[48]

Previous research on military assistance tended to focus on arms transfers—FMS rather than the concessional programs examined in this study—especially during the Cold War. Scholars found that arms transfers to developing countries during the Cold War increased the likelihood of coups and the length of military regimes,[49] promoted regional arms races,[50] and had varying success in influencing recipient state policy.[51]

There is an extensive literature on the impact of development aid, but there is little consensus regarding a positive relationship between development aid and growth or stability. Some studies indicate that economic aid has no effect (or an ambiguous effect) on growth and stability,[52] while other studies show that positive effects of aid on

---

[48] Terrence K. Kelly, Jefferson P. Marquis, Cathryn Quantic Thurston, Jennifer D. P. Moroney, and Charlotte Lynch, *Security Cooperation Organizations in the Country Team: Options for Success*, Santa Monica, Calif.: RAND Corporation, TR-734-A, 2010; Jennifer D. P. Moroney, Joe Hogler, Jefferson P. Marquis, Christopher Paul, John E. Peters, and Beth Grill, *Developing an Assessment Framework for U.S. Air Force Building Partnerships Programs*. Santa Monica, Calif.: RAND Corporation, MG-868-AF, 2010.

[49] Edward Thomas Rowe, "Aid and Coups d'Etat: Aspects of the Impact of American Military Assistance Programs in the Less Developed Countries," *International Studies Quarterly*, Vol. 18, No. 2, June 1974, pp. 239–255; Talukder Maniruzzaman, "Arms Transfers, Military Coups, and Military Rule in Developing States," *Journal of Conflict Resolution*, Vol. 36, No. 4, December 1, 1992, pp. 733–755.

[50] Gregory S. Sanjian, "Promoting Stability or Instability? Arms Transfers and Regional Rivalries, 1950–1991," *International Studies Quarterly*, Vol. 43, No. 4, December 1999, pp. 641–670.

[51] John Sislin, "Arms as Influence: The Determinants of Successful Influence," *Journal of Conflict Resolution*, Vol. 38, No. 4, December 1, 1994, pp. 665–689.

[52] Raghuram G. Rajan and Arvind Subramanian, "Aid and Growth: What Does the Cross-Country Evidence Really Show?" working paper, National Bureau of Economic Research, 2005.

growth can be seen after a considerable amount of time, such as ten years,[53] and may depend on regime type.[54]

The research on development aid and conflict is similarly inconclusive. Some scholars argue that economic aid can affect the probability of conflict in unstable regions, promoting arms races when aid is not coupled with economic reform policies in the receiving country,[55] having a distorting effect of allowing aid-receiving states to finance military spending,[56] and increasing the risk of civil conflict following severe decreases in aid.[57] Other studies indicate that economic aid may decrease the duration of ongoing conflicts[58] and the likelihood of conflict during a period of democratization.[59] Aggregate economic aid does not appear to increase prospects for democratization,[60] but targeted

---

[53] Michael A. Clemens, Steven Radelet, Rikhil R. Bhavnani, and Samuel Bazzi, "Counting Chickens When They Hatch: Timing and the Effects of Aid on Growth," *Economic Journal*, Vol. 122, No. 561, June 2012, pp. 590–617; Camelia Minoiu and Sanjay G. Reddy, "Development Aid and Economic Growth: A Positive Long-Run Relation," *The Quarterly Review of Economics and Finance*, Vol. 50, No. 1, February 2010, pp. 27–39.

[54] Stephen Kosack, "Effective Aid: How Democracy Allows Development Aid to Improve the Quality of Life," *World Development*, Vol. 31, No. 1, January 2003, pp. 1–22.

[55] Paul Collier and Anke Hoeffler, "Unintended Consequences: Does Aid Promote Arms Races?" *Oxford Bulletin of Economics and Statistics*, Vol. 69, No. 1, 2007, pp. 1–27.

[56] Collier and Hoeffler, 2007.

[57] Richard A. Nielsen, Michael G. Findley, Zachary S. Davis, Tara Candland, and Daniel L. Nielson, "Foreign Aid Shocks as a Cause of Violent Armed Conflict," *American Journal of Political Science*, Vol. 55, No. 2, 2011, pp. 219–232.

[58] J. De Ree, and E. Nillesen, "Aiding Violence or Peace? The Impact of Foreign Aid on the Risk of Civil Conflict in Sub-Saharan Africa," *Journal of Development Economics*, Vol. 88, No. 2, 2009, pp. 301–313.

[59] Burcu Savun and Daniel C. Tirone, "Foreign Aid, Democratization, and Civil Conflict: How Does Democracy Aid Affect Civil Conflict?" *American Journal of Political Science*, Vol. 55, No. 2, April 2011, pp. 233–246.

[60] Stephen Knack, "Does Foreign Aid Promote Democracy?" *International Studies Quarterly*, Vol. 48, No. 1, January 29, 2004, pp. 251–266; Simeon Djankov, José Garcia Montalvo, and Marta Reynal-Querol, "The Curse of Aid," *Journal of Economic Growth*, Vol. 13, No. 3, Septembr 2008, pp. 169–194.

democratization programs may be more successful in this context.[61] An interesting line of recent research is the intersection of military and economic aid. One study argues that the sequencing of military and economic aid during and after a civil conflict will affect prospects for growth.[62] A recent microlevel study of military aid to Colombia shows that provision of aid increased the likelihood of paramilitary attacks in provinces with military bases.[63]

The one thing on which there is general agreement is that the costs of conflict outweigh greatly the costs of preventing the conflict. The literature on the costs of conflict shows that aggregated costs of conflict—including lost growth and development, flight of human capital, and the costs of rebuilding—always make prevention a cost-efficient choice from the perspective of a larger public good.[64] However, mobilizing external actors for preventive action is exceedingly difficult in the absence of a clear sign that a conflict is in fact about to take place. This is a collective action problem that underlies the behavior of the international community.

We take the following from our literature review. One, there is a dearth of empirically based studies of security cooperation. Two, there is little agreement on the impact of development aid, but studies do suggest that there is a complex relationship between development aid and conflict. Three, the development aid literature suggests that the effectiveness of aid will be conditional on the type of aid and the country-specific conditions of the recipient. Four, the costs associated with prevention of conflict are less than the costs associated with conflict.

---

[61] Steven E. Finkel, Aníbal Pérez-Liñán, and Mitchell A. Seligson, "The Effects of U.S. Foreign Assistance on Democracy Building, 1990–2003," *World Politics*, Vol. 59, No. 3, April 2007, pp. 404–439.

[62] Ellyn Creasey, Ahmed S. Rahman, and Katherine A. Smith, "Nation Building and Economic Growth," *American Economic Review*, Vol. 102, No. 3, May 2012, pp. 278–282.

[63] Oeindrila Dube and Suresh Naidu, *Bases, Bullets and Ballots: The Effect of U.S. Military Aid on Political Conflict in Colombia*, SSRN eLibrary, January 4, 2010.

[64] Michael E. Brown, and Richard N. Rosecrance, eds., *The Costs of Conflict: Prevention and Cure in the Global Arena*, Lanham, Md.: Rowman & Littlefield Publishers, 1999; Peter Cross ed., *Contributing to Preventive Action*, Baden-Baden: Nomos Verlagsgesellschaft, 1998.

CHAPTER THREE

Statistical Approach to Assessing the Preventive Hypothesis

To assess the preventive hypothesis, we use statistical analyses to establish whether providing SC was correlated with an improvement in partner countries' fragility, and if so, under what conditions the correlation was stronger. Our statistical analyses assess the relationship between SC and partner countries' fragility across 107 countries from 1991 to 2008. In this chapter, we present the methodology we used to conduct our statistical analyses. We discuss the rationale for the time frame included in our analyses and describe how we identified the countries to include in our analyses, how we structured the analyses, how we defined SC and countries' fragility, and what our data sources were. Appendix B provides detailed graphical descriptions of State Fragility Index (SFI) scores, SC by category, development assistance, and conflict over time for all the countries included in our analyses. This chapter outlines our methodology and, as such, describes how we operationalized and then tested the preventive hypothesis. Chapter Four then presents the results of our analyses.

Periods Included in Our Analyses

Our period begins in 1991 to take into account the different form of and the greater reliance on SC since the end of the Cold War. Since 1991, the depth and scope of SC have increased dramatically, with even larger increases since 2001 (see Figure 3.1).[1] The 2008 end date reflects the availability of cross-national data for many of the variables included in the analyses.[2]

Countries Included in Our Analyses

As we noted in Chapter One, the United States provides SC for a variety of reasons (for example, to increase U.S. influence and access and

Figure 3.1
U.S. Security Cooperation, 1991–2008

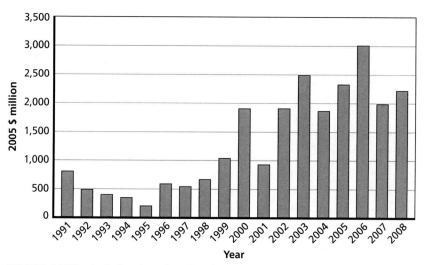

SOURCE: RAND calculations based on data from USAID, 2012; DoD and DoS, various years; Nina M. Serafino, "Department of Defense 'Section 1207' Security and Stabilization Assistance: Background and Congressional Concerns, FY2006–FY2010," Washington, D.C.: Congressional Research Service, RS22871, March 3, 2011; and correspondence with the Center for Hemispheric Defense Studies and the Asia-Pacific Center for Security Studies.
RAND RR350-3.1

---

[1] Figure 3.1 includes data for all countries included in the analyses, as reported in Table 3.1.

[2] The key limiting variable in our analyses is cross-national identification of major episodes of political violence, for which the last year of data is 2008. This variable is discussed in more detail below.

improve interoperability with the partner's forces). Our goal in this project was to focus on whether SC was associated with an improvement in countries' fragility. To do so, we needed to identify a sample of countries in which preventing state instability was likely to be one of the reasons why the United States would provide SC.

To ensure the largest country sample that we could devise, we started with a global sample. We then excluded from our analyses countries for which the decision to provide SC was less likely to be motivated by preventing state instability. Such countries fall into several groups. First, we expect that motivations for SC to countries that involve uniquely important U.S. national interests, such as Iraq, Afghanistan, Egypt, and Israel, differ from those included in our preventive hypothesis. Second, SC to North Atlantic Treaty Organization (NATO) allies reflects a different set of goals, having to do more with alliance commitments and interoperability. Third, we excluded countries with a gross domestic product (GDP) per capita above (2005) $10,000 because we consider these countries to be sufficiently wealthy not to need concessional SC. As a result, given the importance of the preventive hypothesis in U.S. policy, we expect that, if any of the 107 countries included in our sample received SC, the U.S. decision to provide SC would have been motivated at least in part by the goal of reducing the country's fragility.[3] Table 3.1 lists the countries in the dataset that we used for our statistical analysis.

We also excluded observations in which there was incidence of major conflict in the three-year window surrounding the U.S. provision of SC, as we expect that SC in these cases was more likely a response to a crisis rather than an attempt to forestall conflict. We used the Center for Systemic Peace's dataset on Major Episodes of Politi-

---

[3] Of the countries listed in Table 3.1, all but Cuba and Syria received at least one year of SC during the 1992–2003 period. (As will be discussed in detail below, becasue of the lag structure used in this analysis, we assessed the correlation between U.S. SC provided in 1992–2003 and countries' fragility in 1997–2008.) Libya received SC in one year (2000). Iran received SC in 2002 and 2003, and Equatorial Guinea received SC in 2000. The United States also provided SC to China (1995–1997) and Russia (1992–2003). As a sensitivity analysis and to verify that our statistical results were not affected by the inclusion of countries that received little or no SC (Libya, Iran, or Equatorial Guinea), or by Russia or China, we excluded these countries from our analyses. Their exclusion did not affect our results.

Table 3.1
Countries Included in the Analysis

Algeria	Ghana	Oman
Argentina	Guatemala	Pakistan
Armenia	Guinea	Panama
Azerbaijan	Guinea Bissau	Papua New Guinea
Bangladesh	Guyana	Paraguay
Belarus	Haiti	Peru
Benin	Honduras	Philippines
Bhutan	Indonesia	Russia
Bolivia	Iran	Rwanda
Botswana	Jamaica	Saudi Arabia
Brazil	Jordan	Senegal
Burkina Faso	Kazakhstan	Serbia and Montenegro
Burundi	Kenya	Sierra Leone
Cambodia	Kyrgyzstan	Solomon Islands
Cameroon	Laos	South Africa
Central African Rep.	Lebanon	South Korea
Chad	Lesotho	Swaziland
Chile	Liberia	Syria
China	Libya	Tajikistan
Colombia	Macedonia	Tanzania
Comoros	Madagascar	Thailand
Republic of Congo	Malawi	Timor-Leste
Costa Rica	Malaysia	Togo
Cote d'Ivoire	Mali	Trinidad and Tobago
Cuba	Mauritania	Tunisia
Djibouti	Mauritius	Turkmenistan

Table 3.1—Continued

Dominican Republic	Mexico	Uganda
Ecuador	Moldova	Ukraine
El Salvador	Mongolia	Uruguay
Equatorial Guinea	Morocco	Uzbekistan
Eritrea	Mozambique	Venezuela
Ethiopia	Namibia	Vietnam
Fiji	Nepal	Yemen
Gabon	Nicaragua	Zambia
Gambia	Niger	Zimbabwe
Georgia	Nigeria	

cal Violence (MEPV) to identify conflict episodes.[4] Observations are characterized as "in conflict" if there was substantial and prolonged warfare.[5] To assess the sensitivity of our results to the exclusion of these conflict episodes, we reran our analyses including these observations. The results are similar and are reported in Appendix B.

Statistical Estimation Technique

We undertook a time-series cross-sectional analysis of SC to 107 countries from 1991 to 2008. The estimation technique employed was linear regression with a lagged dependent variable, country fixed effects, and robust standard errors.

There are a number of methodological concerns that are inherent in statistical analyses of a large number of countries over time. First, when analyzing relationships over time, it is important to recognize

---

[4]   Monty G. Marshall, *Major Episodes of Political Violence (MEPV) and Conflict Regions, 1946–2008*, Vienna, Va.: Center for Systemic Peace, 2010.

[5]   We identify countries with an MEPV score of 5 and above as "in conflict." Excluding country-years in conflict when SC is provided drops 6 percent of our sample. Results are very similar when these results are included in the analyses.

that what happens in one year is related to what occurred in past years.[6] For example, a country's fragility this year is likely to be similar to its fragility last year. If this intertemporal relationship is not taken into account, statistical analyses may falsely identify relationships between variables, such as an ostensible correlation between receiving SC and an improvement in countries' fragility that in reality was simply a trend in countries' fragility over time. As a result, statistical analysis over time must "detrend" data.

In the results reported here, we used lagged dependent variable models to account for this intertemporal relationship. Lagged dependent variable models include countries' fragility in the prior year as a key predictor of countries' fragility in the current year. This approach detrends the data by explicitly taking into account countries' past performance.

In Appendix B, we report the results of three alternative methods—error correction models, autoregressive models, and dynamic generalized method of moment models—for controlling time-dependence. Error correction models use the year-over-year change in countries' fragility as the dependent variable and include both levels and changes of each of the independent variables. These models isolate the short-term (year-over-year change) and long-term (levels) effects of each of the independent variables. Autoregressive models (Prais-Winston) are a two-stage process in which the temporal dependence of the overall model is estimated in the first stage and controlled for in the second. Dynamic generalized method of moments models (Arellano-Bond) use temporal lags as instrumental variables to account for serial correlation. All three methods for taking into account countries' past performance identify similar correlations between SC and improvement in countries' fragility that we present in Chapter Four. The results from these alternative specifications serve as a sensitivity analysis for our statistical estimator.

Our second methodological concern when undertaking a time-based analysis is to identify the period in which we expect an effect to take place. If SC does increase countries' resilience, any improvement

---

[6]   In more technical terms, we are concerned about serial correlation.

would not be apparent overnight. For example, a recent study of the length of time it takes to observe an impact of foreign aid on economic growth found evidence of a positive relationship between foreign aid and economic growth after ten years.[7] The authors point out that, with respect to economic assistance, it has been difficult to find a positive relationship between aid provision and contemporaneous economic growth. This makes sense, as some aid programs, such as humanitarian assistance, although short term, are not designed to increase economic growth. Others, such as health and infrastructure projects, are designed to increase economic growth but may take longer for their impact to affect economic processes and lead to better economic outcomes. As a result, assessing the impact of economic aid on economic growth over too short a period increases the likelihood that the analysis will find no relationship between aid and growth. To design an assessment of the impact of economic assistance on economic growth, analysts need to identify programs that are designed to increase economic growth and identify the time it will take for the programs to achieve greater economic growth.

Both of these concerns have parallels for this study. We address the choice of programs in the "Security Cooperation" subsection below. With respect to window of time to allow for observation of the impact of SC on countries' fragility, we used a five-year lag structure to assess the impact of SC on countries' fragility. We chose a five-year window, rather than the ten-year window used by Clemens et al., in their analysis of economic development assistance, for two reasons. First, we expect that the lag time to observe the impact of SC on countries' stability will be relatively shorter than that of economic aid on economic growth. Although many SC programs do have a long gestation before results might be evident in a partner country's stability, most SC programs target a shorter window for success than do longer-term economic development projects. Second, there is a practical reason, in that we have a relatively short time-series for analysis (1991–2008). The longer the lag structure, the shorter the available period of analysis. The five-year window allows a sufficiently long time in which to

---

[7] Clemens et al., 2012.

expect SC to have an impact on countries' fragility while maintaining a 13-year period in which to assess countries' shifts in fragility. As a result, we assessed the impact of SC provided between 1991 and 2003 on countries' fragility between 1996 and 2008. To assess the sensitivity of our results to the five-year window, we used three- and seven-year lag structures. The results from the three- and seven-year lag structures were similar to, but somewhat weaker than, the five-year lag structure reported below, suggesting that five years may be an effective period in which to assess the impact of SC on countries' fragility.[8] The results for the three- and seven-year lag structures are reported in Appendix B.

Finally, the countries included in the analyses vary across a wide range of characteristics, such as region, regime type, and level of wealth. To account for the diversity of countries, we included country fixed effects, in which a separate parameter is estimated for each country included in the analyses. We also included country-specific indicators to take into account other factors that might affect countries' fragility, which we discuss below.

Country Characteristics That May Affect State Fragility

SC is not the only factor that affects countries' stability. To focus on the correlation between receiving SC and an improvement in countries' fragility, we included an array of country characteristics that are also expected to change states' fragility in our statistical analyses. Including these variables in our analyses allowed us to more accurately isolate the correlation of SC and an improvement in countries' fragility from correlations with other factors related to countries' fragility.

We included countries' political regime type because previous research has found that full democracies and full autocracies tend to be more resilient than intermediate regimes that include both democratic

---

[8]   The magnitudes of the correlation of SC and state fragility in the three- and seven-year lag structures are 80 percent of the size of those reported in five-year lag structure models and are statistically significant.

and autocratic components.[9] Similarly, countries whose neighbors are involved in armed conflict are more likely to experience domestic instability than are countries in neighborhoods with no conflict. To control for this effect, we included a variable that captures the percentage of a country's neighbors experiencing armed conflict.[10]

We also included U.S. economic assistance and official development assistance from other Organization for Economic Cooperation and Development (OECD) countries to control for the effect of economic assistance on countries' fragility.[11] These economic flows include a wide range of financial aid to countries, ranging from short-term humanitarian assistance to long-term loan funding for infrastructure projects. Countries that receive large infusions of foreign capital may be able to harness this capital to improve their stability. If so, then not controlling for these effects will bias our results on the correlations between SC and improvements in countries' fragility. However, because of the heterogeneous nature of the programs and goals aggregated by these variables, we caution against interpreting the coefficients of these variables as an assessment of the correlation between international development assistance and states' fragility. An assessment of the relationship between international development assistance and state fragility was beyond the scope of this project.

---

[9] Jack A. Goldstone, Robert H. Bates, David L. Epstein, Ted Robert Gurr, Michael B. Lustik, Monty G. Marshall, Jay Ulfelder, and Mark Woodward, "A Global Model for Forecasting Political Instability," *American Journal of Political Science*, Vol. 54, No. 1, January 2010, pp. 190–208.

[10] This variable is coded based on neighborhood conflict data reported in the Major Episodes of Political Conflict Dataset (Marshall, 2010).

[11] We measured U.S. economic assistance as the total amount of assistance reported in the USAID Greenbook minus the accounts included in the Greenbook that we included in our SC measure. Official development assistance from other OECD countries was coded as total gross disbursements minus U.S. gross disbursement. Data are from OECD, Development Assistance Committee data, undated.

State Fragility

To assess whether there is a correlation between receiving SC and an improvement in countries' fragility, we used the SFI as our dependent variable to identify a country's risk of domestic instability. SFI is a 26-point index developed by the Center for Systemic Peace (CSP) to measure countries' fragility.[12] As countries' fragility increases, their probability of domestic instability increases. The index is an aggregate score based on countries' security, political, economic, and social effectiveness and legitimacy. Table 3.2 presents SFI's eight component dimensions and the underlying data used to create the scores in each dimension. For each dimension, CSP created a categorical variable to capture countries' fragility along that dimension.[13] An extremely fragile state (in effect, a failed state) would receive a score of 25 (e.g., Somalia received a score of 25 in 2008). An extremely robust state would receive a score of 0 (e.g., Costa Rica in 2008). Figure 3.2 provides a graphical representation of countries' SFI score in 2010, the most recent year for which data are available.

Table 3.2
State Fragility Index Dimensions

Dimension	Measure
Security effectiveness	Total residual war
Security legitimacy	State repression
Political effectiveness	Regime/governance stability
Political legitimacy	Regime/governance inclusion
Economic effectiveness	GDP per capita
Economic legitimacy	Share of export trade in manufactured goods
Social effectiveness	Human development indicators
Social legitimacy	Infant mortality

---

[12] Marshall and Cole, 2009a, pp. 21–22.

[13] Each dimension has four categories (0–3), except economic effectiveness, which has five (0–4). The scores are equally weighted in the aggregation.

Figure 3.2
State Fragility Index Data from 2010

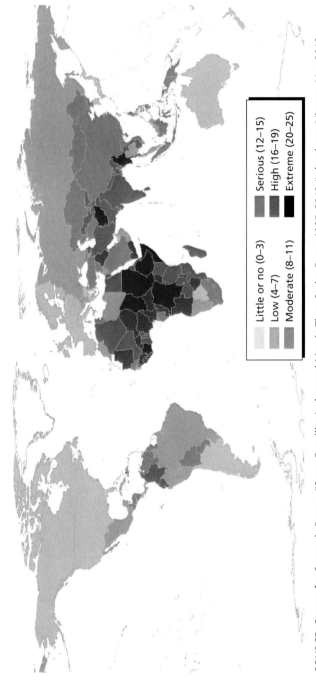

SOURCE: Center for Systemic Peace, "State Fragility Index and Matrix Time-Series Data, 1995–2012," database, Vienna, Va., 2012.

RAND *RR350-3.2*

As Figure 3.3 indicates, SFI provides a wide and well-balanced range of variation in state fragility across the range of observations included in our analyses.

We chose SFI based on both the close fit conceptually between state fragility as defined by CSP and the probability of an adverse outcome in our countries of interest and on the comprehensiveness of SFI's coverage of countries over time. We compared SFI with alternative measures for state fragility, listed in Table 3.3.[14] These alternative indices are similar to SFI in their multidimensional definitions of state fragility. They differed in their reliance on observable country indicators versus subject-matter expert coding of countries. All the measures were highly correlated. Of all the measures, SFI had the greatest spatial

Figure 3.3
Distribution of State Fragility Index, 1991–2008

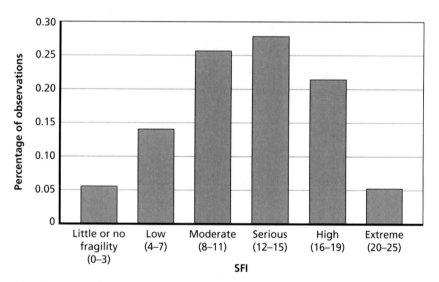

SOURCES: Center for Systemic Peace, 2012, and RAND calculations.
RAND RR350-3.3

---

[14] See Javier Fabra Mata and Sebastian Ziaja, "User's Guide on Measuring Fragility," Oslo, Norway: United Nations Development Programme, 2009, for an excellent and comprehensive review of state fragility indices. We drew heavily on Mata and Ziaja's review for our comparison of state fragility indices.

Table 3.3
State Fragility Indexes

Index	Organization	Source	Dimensions	Start Date	Data Type	Correlation with SFI
SFI	CSP	Marshall and Cole, "State Fragility Index and Matrix 2009," Vienna, Va.: Center for Systemic Peace, 2009b.	Security Political Economic Social	1995	Expert data, public statistics	1.00
BTI State Weakness Index	Bertelsmann Stiftung	Bertelsmann Stiftung, "Transformation Index," web page, 2012.	Security Political	2003	Expert survey	0.81
CIFP Fragility Index	Carleton University	Carleton University, "Country Indicators for Foreign Policy (CIFP)," website, undated.	Security Political Economic Social Environment	2007	Expert data, public statistics	0.89
Country Policy and Institutional Assessment	World Bank	The World Bank, "World Databank: Country Policy and Institutional Assessment," database, 2013.	Political Economic Social	2005	Expert survey	0.92
Failed States Index	Fund for Peace and Foreign Policy	Fund for Peace and Foreign Policy, "Failed States Index," database, 2012.	Security Political Economic Social	2005	Content analysis, expert survey, public statistics	0.86
Global Peace Index	Institute for Economics and Peace	Institute for Economics and Peace, "Global Peace Index," 2013.	Security	2007	Expert data, opinion polls, public statistics	0.76

Table 3.3—Continued

Index	Organization	Source	Dimensions	Start Date	Data Type	Correlation with SFI
Index of State Weakness	Brookings Institution	Susan E. Rice and Stewart Patrick, *Index of State Weakness in the Developing World,* Washington, D.C.: Brookings Institution, 2008.	Security Political Economic Social	2008	Expert data, opinion polls, public statistics	0.89
Peace and Conflict Instability Ledger	University of Maryland	J. Joseph Hewitt, Jonathan Wilkenfeld, and Ted Robert Gurr, "Peace and Conflict 2012," Boulder, Colo: Paradigm Publishers, 2012.	Security Political Economic Social	2003	Expert data, public statistics	0.66
Political Instability Index	Economist Intelligence Unit	The Economist Intelligence Unit, "Social Unrest," web page, 2013.	Political Economic Social	2007	Expert data, opinion polls, public statistics	0.72
Worldwide Governance Indicators: Political Stability and Absence of Violence	World Bank	The World Bank, "Worldwide Governance Indicators," web page, 2013.	Security	1996	Expert data, public statistics	0.78

SOURCE: Mata and Ziaja, 2009, and RAND analysis.

and temporal coverage, making it the most suitable measure for this analysis.

Analyzing aggregate quantitative social scientific data makes it possible to undertake important cross-national comparisons. However, unlike such disciplines as physics or engineering, in which data may be generated and collected in controlled settings, social science data are inherently more imprecise in their measurement, a factor that must be taken into account when interpreting quantitative analyses and when justifying the use and aggregation of social scientific data.

In constructing SFI, CSP endeavored to create a multidimensional measure of state fragility that was comparable across countries and across time. The utility of this measure rests on the assumptions that each of its eight dimensions was "created equal" and that variation across and within each dimension has essentially the same impact on countries' risk of state failure. This is a strong assumption and a gold standard that social scientific indices in general, and state performance indices in particular, are unable to meet in reality.[15]

However, one point that emerges from our analysis of alternative measures of state fragility is the consensus that states' stability is multidimensional. Measures that do not take into account countries' security, political, economic, and social conditions are likely to miss important vulnerabilities. This consensus highlighted the importance of using a multidimensional measure for state fragility for this project. In using SFI, we wanted to make certain that our results reflected countries' overall risk of state failure rather than the overriding effect of only one of the eight dimensions included in SFI.[16] Therefore, to address the concern that CSP's aggregation strategy may have violated the assumption that each of its eight underlying dimensions was independent in a manner that would affect our results meaningfully, we reran our analyses excluding each dimension individually. The results are comparable to those using the entire index and are reported in

[15] Francisco Gutierrez, Diana Buitrago, Andrea Gonzalez, and Camila Lozano, *Measuring Poor State Performance: Problems, Perspectives and Paths Ahead*, London: Crisis States Research Centre, 2011.

[16] We address the potential nonlinearity of SFI substantively in Chapter Four.

Appendix B. These models constitute an analysis of the sensitivity of our results to the inclusion of each of SFI's eight component parts.

Security Cooperation

To construct a dataset on U.S. SC to partner countries since 1991, our first task was to identify SC programs and match them with expenditure data on how much money was spent through each program on each partner country every year. Our second task was to create a measure that was comparable across the countries included in our analyses.

Security Cooperation Programs

We identified SC programs based on two SC "primers" and interviews with practitioners.[17] For the purpose of this analysis, we focused on concessional SC programs (i.e., assistance, not sales). Table 3.4 includes a description of each of the SC programs included in the dataset.

We compiled SC data on the basis of several sources ranging from the USAID Greenbook to cost analyses from individual DoD Regional Centers.[18] The USAID Greenbook's remit is to collect data on all U.S. foreign assistance, including military assistance. The Greenbook includes almost all U.S. SC assistance provided to partner states.[19] However, it is missing programs that are relatively recent in origin, such as Building Partner Capacity of Foreign Militaries (Section 1206) and some DoD programs that focus primarily on education, such as the DoD Regional Centers for Security Studies.[20]

---

[17] Jennifer D. P. Moroney, Joe Hogler, Lianne Kennedy-Boudali, and Stephanie Pezard, *Integrating the Full Range of Security Cooperation into Air Force Planning: An Analytic Primer,* Santa Monica, Calif.: RAND Corporation, TR-974-AF, 2011.

[18] USAID, 2012. Additional information for the Center for Hemispheric Defense Studies and the Asia-Pacific Center for Security Studies was provided through private correspondence.

[19] Greenbook figures account for 99 percent of SC dollar amounts that we identify.

[20] Greenbook does include information on International Military Education and Training (IMET).

Table 3.4
U.S. Security Cooperation Programs Included in the Analysis

Program	Description[a]	Data Source	Amount per Program, 1991–2008[b] ($M)
FMFP[c]	Congressionally appropriated grants and loans, which enable eligible foreign governments to purchase U.S. defense articles, services, and training through either FMS or direct commercial sales.	USAID Greenbook	80,082
Nonproliferation, Antiterrorism, Demining, and Related	Appropriated grant program administered by DoS authorized by Part II, Chapters 8 and 9 of the Foreign Assistance Act, and Section 504 of the FREEDOM Support Act. Section 23, Arms Export Control Act, for Nonproliferation, Antiterrorism, Demining, and Related focuses on demining activities, the clearance of unexploded ordnance, the destruction of small arms, border security, and related activities. Related defense articles, services, and training can be provided through this program. U.S. funding support for the International Atomic Energy Agency and the Comprehensive Nuclear Test Ban Treaty Preparatory Commission is provided through this program.	USAID Greenbook	21,568
International Narcotics Control and Law Enforcement (INCLE)[d]	Appropriated grant program administered by DoS authorized by Section 481, Foreign Assistance Act, to suppress the worldwide illicit manufacture and trafficking of narcotic and psychotropic drugs, money laundering, and precursor chemical diversion, and the progressive elimination of the illicit cultivation of the applicable crops. Recently, the elimination of related narcoterrorism has been included. This program can include the purchase of defense articles, services, and training.	USAID Greenbook	9,977
Drug Interdiction and Counter-Drug Activities	Section 1004 National Defense Authorization Act for FY 1991 (NDAA), P.L. 101-510, authorizes counternarcotics support to U.S. and foreign counterdrug agencies, to include providing defense services and training in support of DoD-loaned equipment.	USAID Greenbook	3,457

Table 3.4—Continued

Program	Description[a]	Data Source	Amount per Program, 1991–2008[b] ($M)
Excess Defense Articles	Excess defense articles identified by the military department or DoD agency are authorized for sale using the FMS authority in Section 21, Arms Export Control Act, and FMS processes identified within the Security Assistance Management Manual for property belonging to the U.S. government. Prices range from 5 to 50 percent of original acquisition value, depending on the condition of the article. Additionally, Section 516, FAA, authorizes the president to transfer excess defense articles on a grant basis to eligible countries.	USAID Greenbook	1,637
IMET	Grant financial assistance for training in the United States and, in some cases, in overseas facilities to selected foreign military and civilian personnel.	USAID Greenbook	809
Building Partner Capacity of Foreign Militaries (Section 1206)	DoD funding may be used annually to equip, supply, and train foreign military forces (including maritime security forces) to conduct counterterrorism operations or to participate in or support military and stability operations in which U.S. forces are participating.	DoD/DoS[e]	546
Regional Centers for Security Studies	Title 10 authorities and DoD appropriations funded the development of five regional centers for security studies. The centers serve as a mechanism for communicating U.S. foreign and defense policies to international students, a means for countries to provide feedback to the United States concerning these policies and communicating country policies to the United States. The regional centers' activities include education, research, and outreach. They conduct multilateral courses in residence; seminars within their regions; and conferences that address global and regional security challenges, such as terrorism and proliferation. Participants are drawn from the civilian and military leadership of allied and partner nations. The Regional Centers for Security Studies are: the George C. Marshall European Center for Security Studies, the Asia-Pacific Center for Security Studies, the William J. Perry Center for Hemispheric Defense Studies, the Africa Center for Strategic Studies, and the Near East South Asia Center for Strategic Studies.	Foreign Military Training Report, APCSS,[f] CHDS[f]	123

Table 3.4—Continued

Program	Description[a]	Data Source	Amount per Program, 1991–2008[b] ($M)
Security and Stabilization Assistance (Section 1207)	Section 1207 of the National Defense Authorization Act for FY2006 (NDAA) authorizes DoD to annually transfer to DoS $100 million in defense articles, services, training or other support for reconstruction, stabilization, and security activities in foreign countries.	CRS[g]	149
Global Peace Operations Initiative (GPOI)	Presidential initiative in coordination with the other G-8 countries to increase the capacity of selected countries to deploy in support of international peace operations.	FMTR	78
Regional Defense Combating Terrorism Fellowship Program	Fellowship program to help key partner nations cooperate with the United States in the fight against international terrorism by providing education and training on a grant basis to foreign military and civilian personnel.	FMTR	68

[a] Descriptions are based on Defense Institute of Security Assistance Management, "The Management of Security Cooperation," Wright Patterson Air Force Base, Ohio, February 2011.

[b] Does not include expenditures in developed countries. Amounts are in 2005 dollars.

[c] The Military Assistance Program (MAP) was merged with FMFP in FY1990. We include MAP expenditures under FMFP.

[d] INCLE includes the Andean Counterdrug Initiative.

[e] Inspectors General, Department of Defense and Department of State, *Interagency Evaluation of the Section 1206 Global Train and Equip Program*, DoD IE-2009-007, August 31, 2009.

[f] The Center for Hemispheric Defense Studies and the Asia-Pacific Center for Security Studies provided additional data for these analyses.

[g] Serafino, 2011.

To address the absence of many of the training programs from the Greenbook, we collected data from the DoD and DoS FMTR.[21] FMTR's remit is to identify foreign training, in terms of both cost and numbers of students trained. FMTR is the most comprehensive source of foreign military training, regardless of what program provided it or who paid for it. However, it does not provide a complete accounting of programs' nontraining expenditures. For example, approximately one-third of GPOI expenditures are training related, while the other two-thirds are spent on deployment, facilities, and equipment costs. FMTR also fails to account for U.S. infrastructure and other supporting costs associated with foreign training, as well as personnel and operational costs for U.S. military forces involved in the training. For example, although reimbursement of some expenses takes place and some training is on a "space available" basis, FMTR does not account for all the additional costs incurred by DoD schoolhouses or training sites for accommodating foreign students. Neither does it account for all the personnel and deployment expenses for U.S. forces providing the training. Nevertheless, we chose the combination of the Greenbook and FMTR as our primary data sources for two reasons: (1) nontraining expenditures, such as those incurred for GPOI, are not directly or primarily in support of prevention goals, such as deploying partner military forces to peacekeeping operations in third countries; (2) data collection for supporting costs would be extremely uneven and difficult to break out by country, thereby creating disparities in the data.

The SC measure excludes programs for which little usable data exist. This includes some training programs, military to military programs, and some military service–specific (including Army-specific) programs (discussed in more detail in Appendix A). The measure also excludes programs that were for countries not included in the analyses (as we noted earlier, these are wealthy countries with a GDP per capita greater than $10,000 [2005], NATO members, Afghanistan, Iraq, Israel, and Egypt). Finally, we excluded programs that do not qualify as SC by our definition. In particular, we excluded nonconcessional sales

---

[21] Department of Defense and Department of State, *Foreign Military Training,* Vol. I, joint report to Congress, fiscal years 1999–2011.

of military training and equipment, economic development assistance, and peacekeeping operations.

Security Cooperation Comparability Across Countries

Figure 3.4 presents the distribution of country-year observations in our analyses by amount of SC provided. The y-axis captures the percentage of the observations each bar represents, and the x-axis captures the range of SC expenditures each bar represents. As Figure 3.4 shows, there is a large dispersion in the amount of SC provided across country-year observations. Between 1991 and 2008, 15 percent of the country-year observations in our dataset received no SC, while Colombia and

Figure 3.4
Distribution of Magnitude of U.S. Security Cooperation by Country-Year Observations, 1991–2008

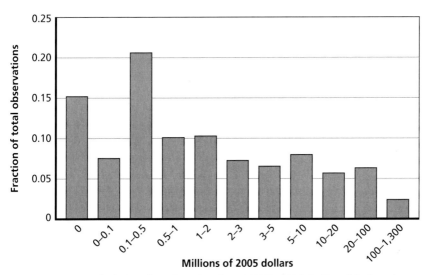

SOURCES: RAND calculations based on data from USAID, 2012; DoD and DoS, various years; Serafino, 2011; and correspondence with the Center for Hemispheric Defense Studies and the Asia-Pacific Center for Security Studies.
NOTES: The x-axis depicts the magnitude of SC in country-year observations. The amount included in each bar increases from left to right to account for the large number of country-year observations in the sample that receive small amounts of SC and the small number of observations that receive large amounts of SC. The y-axis is the fraction of country-year observations included in each bar.
RAND RR350-3.4

Jordan received on average \$422 million and \$169 million annually, respectively. Two factors drive this dispersion. First, all else equal, larger countries tend to receive larger amounts of SC. Second, some countries, such as Jordan or Colombia, receive larger amounts of SC than other countries.

To increase comparability across countries, we undertook two data transformations for SC and all economic assistance data used in our analysis. First, we took into account differences in the size of countries by normalizing financial series based on countries' population to create per capita measures. Given differences in the magnitudes of SC and economic assistance, we used different scales for SC and economic assistance. U.S. economic assistance and official development assistance from other OECD countries is measured in per-person dollars. Because the scale of SC is much smaller than U.S. economic assistance or official development assistance from other OECD countries, the scale for SC is per 10,000 people.

Second, we use a modified logarithm transformation of these data. Foreign assistance data are characterized by a significant percentage of zeroes, capturing country-years in which no aid was provided, and of very large numbers, capturing country-years in which large quantities of assistance were provided. Both these data characteristics are problematic for statistical analyses, and failure to correct for them can lead to biased results.

A common approach to correcting for data with a few very large numbers is to take a standard log transformation.[22] This makes the largest numbers less extreme, making them look more like the numbers in the middle of the distribution. As a result, a one-unit increase at a small value (e.g., 1) has a larger impact than a one unit increase at a large value (e.g., 100). The problem with a standard log transformation, however, is that the log of zero is undefined. If a log transformation is used, either the observations that are zeroes are excluded from the analysis, or they are changed from zero to a small positive value, such as 0.01. Neither of these options is satisfying. Dropping the country-years that received no assistance ignores a very important group of

---

[22] The formula for the standard log transformation is $\log(y_i)$.

countries—the countries that do not receive aid are different from those that do in important ways. Similarly, coding countries as receiving "a little" aid when in fact they did not receive any at all changes the relationship between those that received a small amount of aid and those that received none at all.

Foreign assistance data are very similar to wealth data, in which some people have no wealth holdings, and some people (the 1 percent) have very large wealth holdings. An alternative data transformation approach that is used in studies of wealth data to reduce the dispersion in their data while not losing observations with zero wealth is a modified log transformation, the inverse hyperbolic sine transformation: [23]

$$\log [y_i + (y_i^2 + 1)^{1/2}]$$

Except for very small values, the inverse hyperbolic sine transformation is almost identical to a log transformation. In contrast to a log transformation, however, the inverse hyperbolic sine transformation is defined for zero. As a result, this transformation can be used without having to "fix" the zeroes. Due to its success at reducing data dispersion while also preserving observations that are zero, we used this modified log transformation (the inverse hyperbolic sine transformation) rather than a log transformation in our analyses.

In sum, we used a modified logarithmic transformation of 2005 dollars SC expenditures per 10,000 people to measure SC in our statistical analyses.

---

[23] For discussion, see John B. Burbidge, Lonnie Magee, and A. Leslie Robb, "Alternative Transformations to Handle Extreme Values of the Dependent Variable," *Journal of the American Statistical Association*, Vol. 83, No. 401, March 1988, pp. 123–127.

CHAPTER FOUR
Assessing the Preventive Hypothesis

In this chapter, we assess the preventive hypothesis through a statistical analysis of U.S. security assistance to 107 countries from 1991–2008. Our results identify a correlation between U.S. SC and improved stability in partner countries. The strength of this correlation depends on the partner country's domestic characteristics. In particular, our results suggest that, on average, provision of SC was more highly correlated with an improvement in partner countries' fragility in countries that were more democratic and that started off with stronger state capacity. These results comport well with SC provision from 1991–2003, during which time very little SC went to the least democratic or the most fragile countries.

We also found that not all types of SC were equally correlated with improvements in partner countries' fragility. In particular, we found that SC directed at building partner capacity (education and building counternarcotics and law enforcement capabilities) was more highly correlated with reducing recipients' fragility than Foreign Military Finance (FMF) expenditures.[1] This may reflect the use of FMF to accomplish other goals, such as increasing access, strengthening interoperability, and building relationships.

This chapter discusses our findings. We end the chapter with an interpretation of the results.

---

[1] FMF is the largest concessional SC program. It is used to finance, through grants or loans, the acquisition of U.S. military articles, services, and training.

SC Is Correlated with Improvements in Countries' Stability

The preventive hypothesis, as elucidated in DoD policy, assumes that U.S. SC efforts will lead to stronger host-state institutions and make countries less fragile. If the preventive hypothesis is true, there should be a positive correlation between U.S. provision of SC and an improvement in partner countries' stability. We expect that receiving SC is associated with a decline in countries' fragility five years later, all else equal. We tested for this relationship in Model 1, "SC and SFI," which is reported in Table 4.1.[2] As discussed in detail in Chapter Three, Model 1 is a time-series cross-sectional linear regression model with a lagged dependent variable, country fixed effects, and robust standard errors. The dependent variable is countries' SFI score, and our key independent variable is SC five years prior. Model 1 also includes U.S. economic assistance, official development assistance from non-U.S. OECD countries, conflict in neighboring countries, and a series of political regime–type variables to take into account other factors that affect state fragility.

Model 1, "SC and SFI," provides support for the preventive hypothesis. SC is correlated with an improvement in countries' stability. Substantively, receiving $1,000 per 10,000 people in SC was associ-

---

[2] The results presented in Table 4.1 for Model 1, and for all subsequent models, are the statistical output from the regression model. The variables included in the model are listed in the first column. For each variable included in the model two numbers are reported. The first value is the variable's coefficient, which is the predicted marginal effect of a one-unit increase in the variable on the dependent variable (e.g., countries' SFI scores). The coefficient represents a single point prediction; however, all predictions entail uncertainty. Thus, the second value, which is reported in parentheses, is the standard error of the coefficient. The standard error determines the confidence level of the predicted marginal effect of the variable. The larger the standard error, the less precise the predicted marginal effect. Taken together, the coefficient and the standard error allow assessment of statistical significance. An effect is considered statistically significant if the upper bound and the lower bound of the estimated effect are both above (or both below) zero. If a variable is statistically significant at the 90-, 95- or 99-percent level, we denote this by including a *, **, or *** next to the coefficient, respectively. To provide a more accessible format for interpreting the model results, we also present our results graphically.

Table 4.1
Results for Model 1: SC and SFI

Variable	Model 1	
SFI, one year prior	0.70 (0.03)	***
SC per 10,000 people, five years prior	−0.04 (0.01)	***
U.S. economic assistance per capita, five years prior	−0.02 (0.05)	
Official development aid from non-U.S. OECD countries per capita, five years prior	0.13 (0.05)	**
Conflict in neighboring countries	0.28 (0.18)	
Full autocracy	0.57 (0.40)	
Partial autocracy	0.93 (0.40)	**
Partial democracy	0.28 (0.35)	
Factional democracy	1.01 (0.37)	***
Constant	2.69 (0.44)	***
R²	0.58	
Number of observations	1,262	

SOURCE: RAND analysis.
NOTES: Standard errors in parentheses. * p < 0.1, ** p < 0.05, *** p < 0.01.

ated with an approximately 0.34-point decline in SFI on average.[3] This is shown graphically in Figure 4.1. The thick middle line represents

---

[3] $1,000 per 10,000 people represents the 44th percentile of SC expenditure in the sample. The median amount of SC from the United States for our sample was $1,447 per 10,000 people. The marginal effect of a variable is based on its model coefficient (the coefficient for SC in Model 1 is −0.045) multiplied by the amount of the variable. Therefore, the marginal effect of 1 SC is −0.04. To calculate the marginal effect of $1,000 SC per 10,000,

Figure 4.1
Marginal Effect of SC on Countries' SFI as SC Expenditures Increase

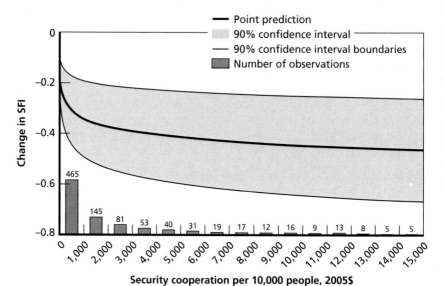

Security cooperation per 10,000 people, 2005$

SOURCE: RAND calculations.

RAND RR350-4.1

Model 1's prediction of the marginal effect of SC on a country's SFI score.[4] The thinner lines represent the 90-percent confidence interval. Taken together, these three lines illustrate Model 1's predicted size of the correlation between SC and countries' improvement in their SFI scores and the range of values within which we are 90 percent certain the correlation between SC and SFI resides.

As Figure 4.1 shows, based on the results in Model 1, larger amounts of SC were associated with larger declines in countries' fra-

---

we needed to transform 1,000 into a modified log transformation as described in Chapter Three that is used to create the SC variable (7.6). Based on this, the marginal effect of $1,000 SC per 10,000 people on a country's SC score, based on Model 1, is 7.6 multiplied by −0.045, which equals −0.34. Recalling that lower SFI scores represent less fragility, this means that based on the results in Model 1, $1,000 SC per 10,000 is correlated with a 0.34-point improvement in countries' SFI scores.

[4]   The marginal effect captures the change in SFI associated with providing SC, holding all other factors constant.

gility. However, the marginal increase in countries' stability associated with larger amounts of SC tapers off rapidly. While $1,000 per 10,000 people in SC was correlated with a 0.34-point decline in SFI, $15,000 per 10,000 people was correlated with only a 0.46-point decline in recipients' SFI scores.[5]

The bars at the bottom of Figure 4.1 depict the distribution of SC expenditures in our sample. The number above each bar is the number of country-year observations that fall within each $1,000 range along the x-axis. For example, 465 country-year observations received between $1 and $1,000. This distribution demonstrates that the majority of SC expenditures are less than $1,000 per 10,000 people and that there are a few very large SC expenditures. Based on the results from Model 1 and the pattern of SC between 1992 and 2003, most U.S. SC expenditures occurred in the range where SC was most highly correlated with improvements in partner countries' SFI scores.

SC is not the only variable to affect countries' fragility. We included full autocracy, partial autocracy, partial democracy, and factional democracy (with full democracy as the excluded category to which these four regime types are compared) to account for the correlation between countries' regime type and changes in their fragility. Based on the coefficients reported in Model 1, partial autocracies and highly factional democracies are correlated with greater state fragility than are full democracies. Partially democratic regimes and fully autocratic regimes were no more correlated with state fragility than were fully democratic regimes. Conflict in a country's neighborhood was correlated with greater state fragility, although the effect was not statistically significant. State fragility in the current year is highly correlated with state fragility in the prior year.

---

[5] One concern that arises from Figure 4.1 is that the flatness of the relationship between SC and SFI might be an artifact of the logged scale for SFI. We addressed this concern by rerunning Model 1 including SC squared, which is SC times SC (Appendix B). Including SC squared allowed us to identify whether the correlation between SC and improvements in countries' SFI scores was larger or smaller for larger or smaller amounts of SC. The results from this model are almost identical to those reported in Model 1, providing further support for the relationship depicted in Figure 4.1.

$15,000 per 10,000 people represents the 91st percentile of the sample; 18 percent of the observations in the sample received no SC.

The relationship between international economic assistance and fragility across our analyses was inconclusive.[6] In Model 1, U.S. economic assistance appeared to have no correlation with states' fragility. In contrast, official development assistance from other OECD countries was associated with worsening SFI scores. In general, these results are in keeping with the inconclusive results found in the research community with respect to the relationship between development assistance and its effect on recipient countries' economic growth and stability.[7] There are also more-specific explanations for these results in our model specification.

First, the five-year lag structure adopted in this analysis for SC may be too short to assess the impact of development assistance effectively.[8] As a further exploration of the relationship between economic assistance and state fragility, we reran Model 1 including ten-year lags for official development assistance from other OECD countries and U.S. development assistance. This model is reported in Appendix B. Taking into account a ten-year lag, official development assistance from other OECD countries was associated with greater state resilience, and just missed statistical significance at the 90-percent level. However, the effect of U.S. economic assistance remained statistically insignificant.

Second, the lack of support for U.S. economic assistance also may reflect the aggregate nature of the variable used in this analysis to capture other U.S. aid rather than the lack of a relationship between U.S. economic assistance and state resilience. For example, the USAID Greenbook includes such budget items as "Operating Expenses of the USAID" and "Payment to the Foreign Service Retirement and Disability Fund, USAID" in its calculation of the economic assistance that countries receive from the United States. With respect to this analysis,

---

[6] Across all the models in our analyses, international aid was sometimes correlated with increased fragility. U.S. aid was sometimes correlated with decreased fragility. In some models, neither international assistance model was correlated with state fragility.

[7] For a recent review, see Joseph Wright and Matthew Winters, "The Politics of Effective Foreign Aid," *Annual Review of Political Science*, Vol. 13, 2010, pp. 61–81.

[8] Given the indirect channels by which development assistance may affect economic growth, Clemens et al., 2012, argues that development aid may have a ten-year lag prior to observing any benefits.

the U.S. economic assistance variable was included to account for all other U.S. expenditures in partner nations so as not to erroneously capture their effects in SC. Therefore, the variable is coded as all other U.S. expenditures included in the USAID Greenbook. While such a measure is important for our analysis of the impact of SC in reducing countries' fragility, it is a poor proxy to assess the direct impact of U.S. economic assistance on countries' fragility, as much of what is included may not have been spent directly on development assistance.

Third, U.S. economic assistance is a broad mix of development and humanitarian assistance.[9] Countries experiencing humanitarian or natural disasters are more likely both to receive economic assistance and to experience an increase in state fragility. Our research approach does not disentangle this contemporaneous effect on the relationship between U.S. international economic assistance and state fragility.

Correlation Between SC and Improvements in Countries' Stability Is Conditional on Partner Country Characteristics

The results reported in Model 1 are based on the average effect of SC on SFI in 107 countries from 1991–2008. Model 1 does not take into account differences in the correlation between SC and improvements in countries' stability based on partner countries' characteristics. However, we would expect that the extent to which U.S. SC efforts lead to stronger host-state institutions and make countries less fragile depends on partner country–specific characteristics. If this is true, the strength of the correlation between U.S. provision of SC and an improvement in partner countries' stability should vary depending on countries' characteristics. In particular, we expect that the correlation between SC and decreased fragility will be conditional on partner states' domestic and regional characteristics and the availability of economic assistance.

---

[9] In FY2011, DoS and USAID spent $2.5 billion on "governing justly and democratically" programs, $10 billion on "investing in people" programs, $4.8 billion on economic growth programs, and $3.8 billion on humanitarian assistance programs. DoS, "Congressional Budget Justification, Foreign Assistance Summary Tables," Fiscal Year 2013, Table 5.

Correlation Between SC and Improvements in Countries' Stability Is Stronger in Less-Fragile Countries

The preventive hypothesis assumes that U.S. SC efforts will lead to stronger host-state institutions and make countries less fragile. However, by its very construction, the preventive hypothesis assumes that there is a state with functioning state institutions that U.S. SC efforts can help to strengthen. In the least capable (and hence most fragile) countries in the world, these preconditions do not exist. As a result, SC should be a less effective policy tool for increasing stability in the least capable states than it should be in more-capable states. With respect to our statistical analysis, a stronger correlation between SC and improvements in state fragility in more-capable countries than in less-capable countries would be evidence in support of this argument.

We examined the impact of state capacity on the correlation between SC and improvements in state fragility in two ways. First, we used countries' SFI scores in the year in which they received SC as a proxy for their state capacity. We assessed the extent to which the correlation between SC and an improvement in countries' SFI scores five years later varied depending on how fragile countries were when they received SC. To do so, we reran Model 1 and included an interaction between SC and countries' SFI scores in the year in which they received SC.[10] We report this as Model 2—"SC and Fragility"—in Table 4.2, and present the results graphically in Figure 4.2.

As Figure 4.2 shows, the correlation between SC and improvements in countries' fragility was stronger for countries that had more-stable starting positions. For a country with an SFI score of 12 (the median score in our sample), $1,000 in SC per 10,000 people were associated with a 0.4-point decline in SFI. In contrast, for the most fragile partner states (SFI scores between 21 and 25), there was no statistically significant correlation between SC and a change in countries'

---

[10] In a regression, an interaction is a variable created by multiplying two variables together. In Model 2, the two uninteracted variables are SC per 10,000 people, 5 years prior and SFI, 5 years prior. The interaction is SC per 10,000 people, 5 years prior * SFI, 5 years prior. Including this interaction allows us to examine whether the relationship between SC and SFI varies at different levels of SFI in the year in which SC was provided. We used multiplicative interactions to assess all the conditional hypotheses presented in this section.

Table 4.2
Results for Model 2: SC and Fragility

Variable	Model 2	
SFI, one year prior	0.59	***
	(0.04)	
SC per 10,000 people, five years prior	−0.07	***
	(0.03)	
SC per 10,000 people, five years prior * SFI, five years prior	0.002	
	(0.002)	
SFI, five years prior	0.04	
	(0.03)	
U.S. economic assistance per capita, five years prior	−0.14	**
	(0.06)	
Development aid from non-U.S. OECD countries per capita, five years prior	0.18	**
	(0.09)	
Conflict in neighboring countries	0.43	
	(0.29)	
Full autocracy	−0.05	
	(0.25)	
Partial autocracy	0.36	
	(0.25)	
Partial democracy	−0.28	***
	(0.09)	
Factional democracy	0.40	**
	(0.19)	
Constant	3.97	***
	(0.53)	
R^2	0.48	
Number of observations	875	

SOURCE: RAND analysis.
NOTES: Standard errors in parentheses. * $p < 0.1$, ** $p < 0.05$, *** $p < 0.01$.

Figure 4.2
Marginal Effect of $1,000 SC per 10,000 People on Countries' SFI as SFI Varies

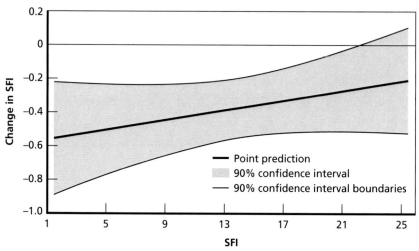

SOURCE: RAND analysis.
RAND RR350-4.2

fragility.[11] The results from Model 2 indicate a correlation between SC and improvement in state fragility for all but the weakest states but that this correlation is stronger in countries with stronger state capacity.

Figure 4.3 displays the total amount of SC spent at different levels of state reach. SC spending patterns appeared to match well with the results from Model 3. Extremely fragile countries (SFI: 21–25), in which SC was not correlated with an improvement in fragility, received low levels of SC, while countries that were less fragile but whose fragility was considered serious (SFI: 12–15) and in which SC was correlated with an improvement in countries' fragility, received the highest levels of SC.

Second, we examined the impact of state capacity on the correlation between SC and improvements in state fragility based on the state's capacity to project its governance functions throughout its terri-

---

[11] The difference between SC effectiveness at the 5th percentile of SFI (4) and the 95th percentile of SFI (21) is 0.24 points, which is statistically significant at the 70-percent level.

Figure 4.3
Total SC by SFI, 1991–2003

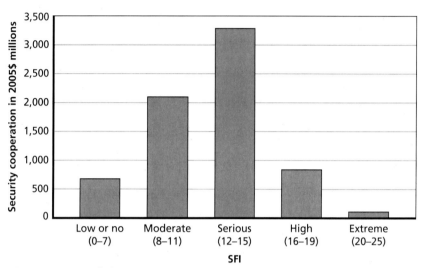

SOURCE: RAND analysis.

RAND RR350-4.3

tory (state reach). Helge Holterman (2012) has identified "state reach" as an important factor for staving off civil war and argues that states that can penetrate their countrysides are more effective in preventing insurgencies.[12] State reach is a three-dimensional index composed of road density, telephone density, and urban population.[13] Holterman's logic behind this measure is twofold. First, governments generally hold the cities, so the more urban the population, the more control the government has of its population. Second, governments are more effective in fighting insurgencies if they can reach and communicate with all

---

[12] Helge Holterman, "Explaining the Development–Civil War Relationship," *Conflict Management and Peace Science*, Vol. 29, No. 1, 2012, pp. 56–78.

[13] State reach ranges from 0 to 100. In our sample, most of the observations fall within the 20–80 range. Median state reach in our sample is 53. Based on the results in Model 3, the marginal effect of SC on SFI was statistically significant for observations with a state reach score of 53 and higher. The difference between SC effectiveness at the 5th percentile of state reach (30) and the 95th percentile of state reach (73) is 0.61 points, which is statistically significant at the 90-percent level.

parts of the country. Countries with better roads and better telecommunications networks provide a better infrastructure with which to fight insurgents.

We assessed the extent to which the correlation between SC and an improvement in countries' fragility varied depending on how comprehensive a country's state reach was. To do so, we reran Model 1 and included an interaction between SC and countries' state reach.[14] We report this as Model 3—"SC and State Reach"—in Table 4.3, and present the results graphically in Figure 4.4.

As Figure 4.4 shows, the correlation between SC and improvements in countries' fragility was stronger for countries that had more state reach than for countries that had less state reach. For a country with a state reach score of 53 (the median score in our sample), $1,000 in SC per 10,000 people was associated with a 0.25-point decline in SFI. In contrast, there is no statistically significant relationship between SC and SFI for countries with lower levels of state reach.

As Figure 4.5 shows, SC expenditures appeared to comport well with the results from Model 3. SC expenditures were much higher in countries with a state reach of 55 or greater. SC to these countries was correlated with an improvement in countries' fragility. In contrast, relatively little SC went to countries with low state reach, in which there was no statistically significant correlation between SC and change in countries' fragility.

The results from Models 2 and 3 present a similar picture. We used both state reach and countries' initial SFI scores as proxy variables for state capacity. These two conditions are closely related. In our sample, countries' state reach and SFI scores correlate at 70 percent. Both models found evidence of a stronger correlation between SC and improvements in countries' fragility in countries with greater state capacity. In both models, there was no statistically significant cor-

---

[14] In a regression, an interaction is a multiplicative variable created by multiplying two variables together. In Model 3, the two uninteracted variables are SC per 10,000 people, 5 years prior, and state reach. The interaction is SC per 10,000 people, 5 years prior * state reach. Including this interaction allows us to examine whether the relationship between SC and SFI varies at different levels of state reach. We use multiplicative interactions to assess all of the conditional hypotheses presented in this section.

Table 4.3
Results for Model 3: SC and State Reach

Variable	Model 3	
SFI, one year prior	0.54	***
	(0.04)	
SC per 10,000 people, five years prior	0.07	
	(0.05)	
SC per 10,000 people, five years prior * state reach	−0.002	*
	(0.001)	
State reach	−0.11	***
	(0.03)	
U.S. economic assistance per capita, five year prior	−0.10	
	(0.07)	
Development aid from non-U.S. OECD countries per capita, five years prior	0.11	
	(0.11)	
Conflict in neighboring countries	0.37	
	(0.32)	
Full autocracy	0.04	
	(0.28)	
Partial autocracy	0.51	**
	(0.23)	
Partial democracy	−0.22	***
	(0.06)	
Factional democracy	0.60	***
	(0.16)	
Constant	10.63	***
	(2.14)	
R^2	0.45	
Number of observations	753	

SOURCE: RAND analysis.
NOTES: Standard errors in parentheses. * $p < 0.1$, ** $p < 0.05$, *** $p < 0.01$.

relation between SC and changes in countries' fragility for the least capable countries.

Figure 4.4
Marginal Effect of $1,000 SC per 10,000 People on Countries' SFI as State Reach Varies

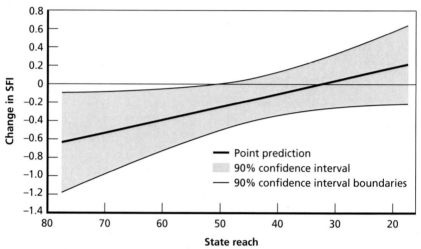

SOURCE: RAND analysis.
NOTE: X-axis ranges from greatest state reach on the left to lowest on the right.
RAND RR350-4.4

Correlation Between SC and Improvements in Countries' Stability Is Strongest in More-Democratic Regimes

We assessed whether the strength of the correlation between SC and improvements in countries' fragility was conditional on regime type. In particular, SC may be more effective in more-democratic countries. If this is true, the correlation between U.S. provision of SC and an improvement in SFI should be stronger for more-democratic countries and weaker for less-democratic countries.

We examined the impact of regime type on the correlation between SC and improvements in state fragility by including interactions between SC and partner countries' political regime type in Model 4—"SC and Regime Type."[15] We report this as Model 4 in Table 4.4, and present the results graphically in Figure 4.6.

---

[15] Because our sample includes only seven cases of full democracies—Chile, Costa Rica, Mauritius, Mongolia, Panama, Trinidad, Tobago, and Uruguay—we were concerned that the results might be sensitive to their inclusion. As a result, we excluded these countries in

Figure 4.5
Total SC by State Reach, 1991–2003

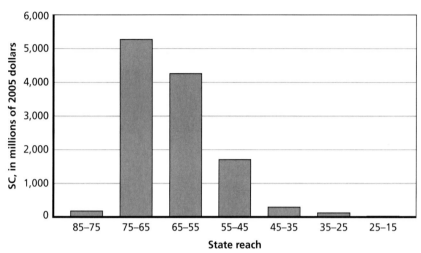

SOURCE: RAND analysis.
NOTE: X-axis ranges from greatest state reach on the left to lowest on the right.
RAND *RR350-4.5*

As Figure 4.6 shows, the correlation between SC and improvements in countries' fragility was stronger for more-democratic regimes; however, the differences across regime types were small and statistically insignificant. In particular, there was no statistically significant correlation between SC and change in countries' fragility in full autocracies. Given the large confidence interval for full autocracies, this null finding may reflect the diversity of countries that are full autocracies and

---

Model 4. For the political regime types included in the sample for Model 4 (full autocracy, partial autocracy, partial democracy, and factional democracy), the excluded political regime category for the model is full autocracy. This means that there is no coefficient reported for full autocracy and the coefficients for partial autocracy, partial democracy, and factional democracy are interpreted relative to the baseline effect of a full autocracy. For interpretation, the coefficient for SC per 10,000 people, 5 years prior captures the marginal effect of SC in full autocracies. The marginal effects for the other political regimes are calculated by adding the coefficient for SC per 10,000 people, 5 years prior * [political regime type] to the coefficient for SC per 10,000 people, 5 years prior, times the size of SC to be provided (7.6, which is the inverse hyperbolic sine transformation for $1,000 for 10,000 people, as discussed in detail in Chapter Three).

Table 4.4
Results for Model 4: SC and Regime Type

Variable	Model 4	
SFI, one year prior	0.70	***
	(0.03)	
SC per 10,000 people, five years prior	−0.03	
	(0.02)	
SC per 10,000 people, five years prior * partial autocracy	−0.01	
	(0.03)	
SC per 10,000 people, five years prior * partial democracy	−0.02	
	(0.03)	
SC per 10,000 people, five years prior * factional democracy	−0.03	
	(0.03)	
U.S. economic assistance per capita, five years prior	−0.03	
	(0.05)	
Development aid from non-U.S. OECD countries per capita, five years prior	0.14	***
	(0.06)	
Conflict in neighboring countries	0.25	
	(0.18)	
Partial autocracy	0.40	
	(0.24)	
Partial democracy	−0.17	
	(0.23)	
Factional democracy	0.59	***
	(0.23)	
Constant	3.30	***
	(0.38)	
R^2	0.58	
Number of observations	1,187	

SOURCE: RAND analysis.
NOTES: Standard errors in parentheses. * $p < 0.1$, ** $p < 0.05$, *** $p < 0.01$.

the diversity of goals the United States has when providing SC to full autocracies. Moreover, relatively little SC went to full autocracies in our sample. Figure 4.7 displays the total amount of SC spent in each type of regime in our sample. SC expenditures appeared to track countries'

Figure 4.6
Marginal Effect of $1,000 per 10,000 People on Countries' SFI as Regime Type Varies

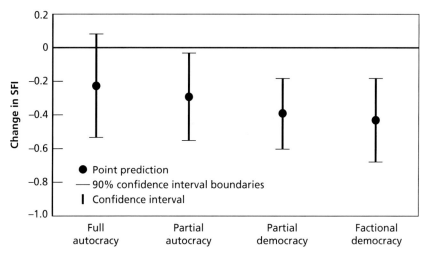

SOURCE: RAND analysis.

RAND *RR350-4.6*

level of democracy. As a whole, factional democracies, the most democratic regimes included in Model 4, received seven times larger levels of SC expenditures than did full autocracies.

One concern arising from these results is that countries' regime types may simply serve as proxies for a different effect. For example, if full autocracies are also more fragile and have lower levels of state reach, Model 4 may replicate the results from Models 2 and 3. This does not appear to be the case, because there is little systematic relationship between fully autocratic regimes and their state fragility or reach—the correlations between full autocracy and state reach and SFI on receipt of SC are 3 percent and 1 percent, respectively.[16] Although regime type does not appear to be a proxy for state institutions, it may

---

[16] Partially autocratic regimes have the highest correlation with state reach and SFI, at 30 percent. The correlation between state reach or SFI and partial or factional democracies is 10 percent or less.

Figure 4.7
Total SC by Regime Type, 1991–2003

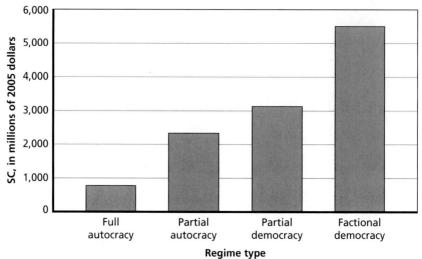

SOURCE: RAND analysis.
RAND *RR350-4.7*

reflect other country characteristics that may affect SC effectiveness. We return to this point below in our regional analysis.

Predicted Correlation Between $1,000 SC per Person and Improvements in Stability Is Based on Countries' State Capacity and Political Regime Type

Taken together, the results from Models 2–4 provide evidence that the correlation between SC and improvements in countries' fragility is stronger in states with greater capacity and more-inclusive political institutions. To illustrate these results, Figure 4.8 combines the predictions from Models 2–4 to create an out-of-sample prediction about the effect of $1,000 SC per 10,000 people per country in 2009.[17] Thus, Figure 4.8 presents a summary prediction about the strength of the

---

[17] An out-of-sample prediction uses the results from analyses conducted on one dataset to make predictions in another dataset. In this instance, we used the results from Models 2–4 generated from our 1991–2008 dataset. We then applied these results to 2009 SFI data that we did not use in our analysis to generate the predictions displayed in Figure 4.8.

Figure 4.8
Predicted Marginal Effect of $1,000 SC per 10,000 on Partner States' SFI in 2009

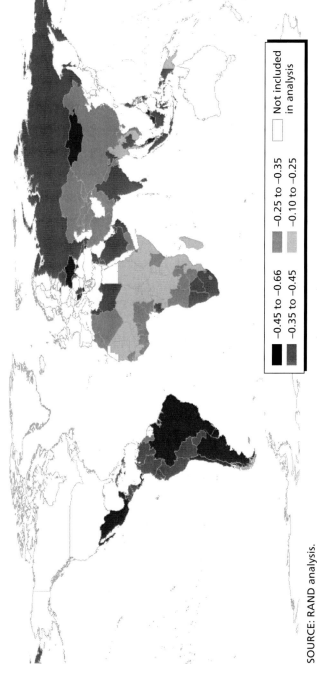

■ −0.45 to −0.66	■ −0.25 to −0.35	□ Not included in analysis
■ −0.35 to −0.45	□ −0.10 to −0.25	

SOURCE: RAND analysis.
NOTES: Values displayed represent the average marginal effect of SC on SFI based on Models 2–4. Data on countries' SFI, regime type and state reach are for 2009.
RAND *RR350-4.8*

correlation between SC and improvements in countries' stability based on 2009 levels of fragility, state reach, and regime type. The darker the country in Figure 4.8, the stronger the predicted correlation between SC and improvements in the country's stability.

Correlation Between SC and Improvements in Countries' Stability Is Strongest in Asia-Pacific, Latin America, and Europe

We also assessed the extent to which the strength of the correlation between SC and improvements in countries' fragility varied across geographic regions. There are many reasons that SC effectiveness may be greater in some regions than others. One, state capacity and political institutions are influenced not only by conditions within countries but also within their regions.[18] For example, the most common political regime type in the Middle East is a full autocracy, and of all the regions examined in this study, Africa has the lowest state reach. Examining SC effectiveness by region rather than by the marginal effect of specific country characteristics may allow an assessment of the joint effect of regionally similar country characteristics that would be overlooked in the marginal, "all-else-equal" analyses undertaken in the previous models. Two, regional differences may reflect the strength of U.S. ties and history within each region. Three, the focus of SC might differ by region, with prevention goals playing a larger role in the use of SC in some regions than in others.

We examined the impact of geographic regions on the correlation between SC and improvements in state fragility by including interactions between SC and countries' region in Model 5—"SC and Region."[19] We report this as Model 5 in Table 4.5 and present the results graphically in Figure 4.9.

---

[18] Kristian Skrede Gleditsch and Michael Ward, "Diffusion and the International Context of Democratization," *International Organization*, Vol. 60, No. 4, October 2006, pp. 911–933.

[19] Countries' regions are based on POLITY's regional groupings. Monty G. Marshall, Ted Robert Gurr, and Keith Jaggers, "POLITY IV Project: Political Regime Characteristics and Transitions, 1800–2009," Dataset Users' Manual, Vienna, Va.: Center for Systemic Peace, 2009. Latin America is the excluded category in Model 5.

Table 4.5
Results for Model 5: SC and Region

Variable	Model 5	
SFI, one year prior	0.69	***
	(0.03)	
SC per 10,000 people, five years prior	−0.08	***
	(0.03)	
SC per 10,000 people, five years prior * Europe	−0.01	
	(0.03)	
SC per 10,000 people, five years prior * Sub-Saharan Africa	0.05	
	(0.03)	
SC per 10,000 people, five years prior * North Africa and Middle East	0.09	**
	(0.04)	
SC per 10,000 people, five years prior * Asia and Pacific	0.02	
	(0.04)	
U.S. economic assistance per capita, five years prior	−0.01	
	(0.05)	
Development aid from non-U.S. OECD countries per capita, five years prior	0.16	***
	(0.06)	
Conflict in neighboring countries	0.22	
	(0.18)	
Full autocracy	0.53	
	(0.41)	
Partial autocracy	0.93	**
	(0.42)	
Partial democracy	0.27	
	(0.36)	
Factional democracy	1.01	***
	(0.38)	
Constant	2.68	***
	(0.44)	
R^2	0.58	
Number of observations	1,262	

SOURCE: RAND analysis.
NOTES: Standard errors in parentheses. * $p < 0.1$, ** $p < 0.05$, *** $p < 0.01$.

Figure 4.9
Marginal Effect of $1,000 SC per 10,000 People on Countries' SFI as Region Varies

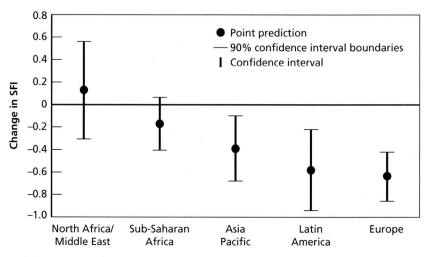

SOURCE: RAND analysis.
RAND RR350-4.9

As Figure 4.9 shows, the correlation between SC and improvements in countries' fragility was stronger in Asia, Latin America, and Europe. There was no statistically significant correlation between SC and change in countries' fragility in Africa or the Middle East. With respect to Africa, these results are consistent with those reported in Models 2–4. Levels of fragility and autocracy were higher throughout Africa than in Asia, Latin America, or Europe. With respect to the results for the Middle East, prevention may have been less of a driver of SC than other U.S. goals, such as increasing U.S. influence and access.

Correlation Between SC and Improvements in Countries' Stability Was Not Conditional on U.S. Economic Assistance

DoD's 2010 QDR highlights the importance of both development and military assistance for building partner capacity in developing countries to prevent and deter conflict.[20] To take into account synergies

---

[20] DoD, 2010.

between SC and U.S. economic assistance, we assessed the extent to which the strength of the correlation between SC and improvements in countries' fragility varied with the amount of international economic assistance a country received.

We examined the impact of U.S. economic assistance on the correlation between SC and improvements in state fragility by including interactions between SC and U.S. economic assistance in Model 6—"SC and U.S. Economic Assistance." We report this as Model 6 in Table 4.6, and present the results graphically in Figure 4.10.

As Figure 4.10 shows, SC was correlated with improvements in countries' fragility regardless of how much U.S. economic assistance was provided. The difference in the strength of the correlation between SC and improvements in countries' fragility as U.S. economic assistance increased was substantively small and statistically insignificant.

Correlation Between SC and Improvements in Countries' Stability Is Conditional on Type of SC

The analyses reported in Models 1–6 examined the correlations between the aggregate amount of SC countries received and improvements in countries' stability. These analyses did not take into account differences in the correlation between SC and improvements in countries' stability based on differences in the type of SC that countries received. We expect that the effect of SC on partner states' fragility will be conditional on the type of SC that is provided.

To assess whether the strength of the correlation between SC and improvements in countries' stability depends on the type of SC that countries received, we disaggregated SC into four categories: FMF, other train and equip (not including FMF), law enforcement and counternarcotics, and education. FMF funds a wide range of training and equipment provided to partner states, but the vast majority of the funds is used for equipment and equipment-related training. Terms for provision of such aid are negotiated between the United States and the partner country. For the most part, other train and equip funds (i.e., nonproliferation, antiterrorism, demining, and related; excess defense

Table 4.6
Results for Model 6: SC and U.S. Economic Assistance

Variable	Model 6	
SFI, one year prior	0.70	***
	(0.03)	
SC per 10,000 people, five years prior	−0.04	**
	(0.02)	
SC per 10,000 people, five years prior * U.S. economic assistance per capita, five years prior	0.00	
	(0.01)	
U.S. economic assistance per capita, five years prior	0.01	
	(0.08)	
Development aid from non-U.S. OECD countries per capita, five years prior	0.14	**
	(0.05)	
Conflict in neighboring countries	0.28	
	(0.19)	
Full autocracy	0.57	
	(0.40)	
Partial autocracy	0.93	**
	(0.40)	
Partial democracy	0.28	
	(0.35)	
Factional democracy	1.01	***
	(0.37)	
Constant	2.63	***
	(0.44)	
R^2	0.58	
Number of observations	1,262	

SOURCE: RAND analysis.
NOTES: Standard errors in parentheses. * $p < 0.1$, ** $p < 0.05$, *** $p < 0.01$.

articles; 1206; 1207; and global peace operations programs) are more narrowly focused than FMF, often on counterterrorism or stabilization missions. Law enforcement and counternarcotics funds (i.e., INCLE and Drug Interdiction and Counter-Drug Activities) are also more narrowly focused than FMF, though activities go beyond simple drug eradication and support many activities that strengthen partner state

Figure 4.10
Marginal Effect of $1,000 SC per 10,000 People on Countries' SFI as U.S.
Economic Assistance Varies

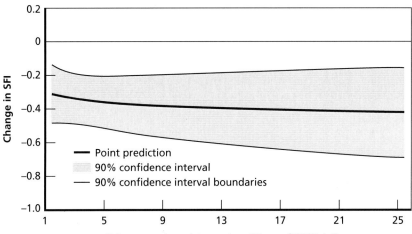

SOURCE: RAND analysis.

RAND *RR350-4.10*

justice sectors and even economic development. Education funds (i.e., International Military Education and Training, Regional Centers, and Regional Defense Combating Terrorism Fellowship Program) focus on human capital development, primarily through schoolhouse instruction and mobile educational and information-sharing events.

We assessed the correlation between SC and improvements in countries' stability depends on the type of SC that countries received by replacing SC with the four SC-type variables (FMF, other train and equip [not including FMF], law Enforcement and counternarcotics, and education) in Model 7—"SC by Type." We report this as Model 7 in Table 4.7, and present the results graphically in Figures 4.11 and 4.12.

As Figure 4.11 shows, there was a strong correlation between SC spent on other train and equip, law enforcement and counternarcotics, and education and improvements in countries' fragility. In contrast, there was no statistically significant correlation between FMF expenditures and change in countries' fragility. The differences in these

Table 4.7
Results for Model 7: SC by Type

Variable	Model 7	
SFI, one year prior	0.68	***
	(0.03)	
FMF per 10,000 people, five years prior	0.00	
	(0.01)	
Other train and equip per 10,000 people, five years prior	−0.03	***
	(0.01)	
Law enforcement and counternarcotics per 10,000 people, five years prior	−0.05	***
	(0.02)	
Education per 10,000 people, five years prior	−0.05	***
	(0.02)	
Other U.S. assistance per capita, five years prior	−0.01	
	(0.05)	
Development aid from non-U.S. OECD countries per capita, five years prior	0.13	**
	(0.05)	
Conflict in neighboring countries	0.24	
	(0.18)	
Full autocracy	0.58	
	(0.41)	
Partial autocracy	0.95	**
	(0.41)	
Partial democracy	0.28	
	(0.36)	
Factional democracy	1.01	***
	(0.39)	
Constant	3.00	***
	(0.46)	
R^2	0.59	
Number of observations	1,262	

SOURCE: RAND analysis.

STANDARD errors in parentheses. * $p < 0.1$, ** $p < 0.05$, *** $p < 0.01$.

Figure 4.11
Marginal Effect of $1,000 SC per 10,000 People on Countries' SFI by SC
Subcategory

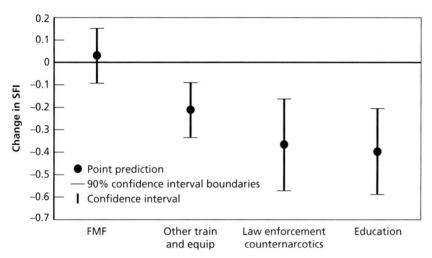

SOURCE: RAND analysis.
RAND RR350-4.11

results across the types of SC may reflect differences in the focus of each SC type and differences in the goals that different SC programs have. In particular, FMF tends to focus primarily on equipment and equipment-based training, often with goals that are not prevention-focused, whereas the other categories are focused primarily on security sector reform, on developing partner-state human capital, or on more-focused, prevention-based training and equipping.

Figure 4.12 replicates the analysis in Figure 4.5 and shows the correlation between each type of SC and change in countries' SFI scores as the amount of SC ranges from 0 to the 90th percentile of expenditures for each SC type. Based on the results shown in panels B, C, and D (in Figure 4.12), larger amounts of other train and equip (not including FMF), law enforcement and counternarcotics, and education were associated with larger declines in countries' fragility. In each case, the marginal increase in countries' stability associated with larger amounts of SC diminished. Having said that, most expenditures in these three categories occurred at the level where an incremental increase in

Figure 4.12
Marginal Effect of SC by Category on Countries' SFI as SC Expenditures Increase

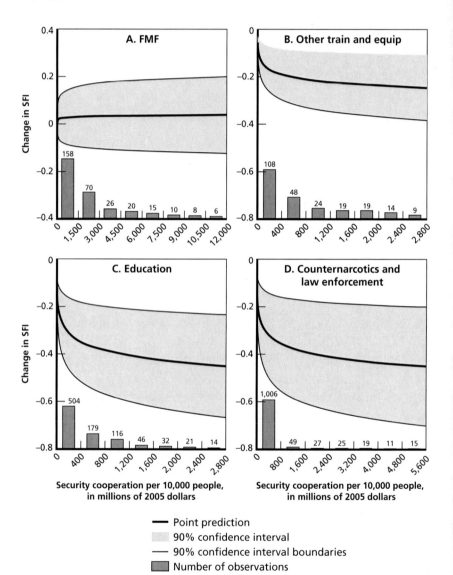

SOURCE: RAND analysis.

SC was associated with the largest incremental decline in countries' fragility—that is, most expenditures occurred prior to the point where the marginal returns curve flattens out and where the marginal return on additional investments is close to zero.

In contrast, the results in panel A in Figure 4.12 show that there was no statistically significant correlation between FMF expenditures and change in countries' fragility regardless of the amount provided. As can be seen in Figure 4.12, FMF also differs from other train and equip (not including FMF), law enforcement and counternarcotics, and education in its distribution of expenditures across country-years. FMF expenditures tend to be much larger on average than the other three types of SC.

CHAPTER FIVE
Findings from Case Studies

The statistical analysis that we discussed in Chapters Three and Four enabled us to show empirically the general patterns in the relationship between the provision of U.S. SC and the target state's fragility. We also conducted a number of case studies to gain insight into how the United States applies SC to individual countries and what it means for a country's SFI score to change. The case studies highlight the fact that the results from the statistical analysis portion of our study cannot be applied to individual countries without additional analysis. The factors that influence SFI scores are complex and involve far more than U.S. SC investments. The case studies are not designed to prove or disprove the results of the statistical study (they cannot do that) but rather to provide context that would otherwise be lacking from a purely statistical analysis. We used the case study approach to assess 12 countries in depth, four of which were examined as pairwise comparisons (i.e., compared to each other). Each case study had the same format and structure.

This chapter summarizes the findings from our case studies. First, we outline the selection criteria for our case studies and present some data for the cases we examined. Then we summarize the findings from the case studies. Finally, we draw some observations from the case study approach for the larger effort of testing the preventive hypothesis.

Case Study Selection and Format

Each case study examined additional details on the kinds of U.S. assistance provided, U.S. government goals vis-à-vis the country, and changes in SFI score. The case studies described similarities to and differences from the overall patterns derived from our statistical analysis, highlighted exogenous events that may have had an effect on the country's fragility, and provided a descriptive assessment of whether and how SC made a difference in that country. The cases focused on the period included in the statistical model—1991 to 2008—but also provided more recent context by addressing activities since the 2008 cutoff date for our statistical analysis.

The cases illustrated the challenges of trying to link different types of analytical approaches. In most cases we examined, SC played an important role in the partner country, but it was not clear to what extent that effect was reflected in SFI scores. The statistical analysis indicated that—accounting for the many other factors that influence SFI scores—there is a statistically significant effect between SC investments and decreased state fragility when aggregated over 1,262 country-year observations. Thus, while the individual country differences provide rich context to help understand how the United States applies SC and how state fragility changes in various situations, these differences also make it difficult to draw specific correlations between SC and that country's changes in SFI. Thus, our statistical analysis provides an aggregated assessment of SC as a preventive tool, and our case studies provide a better understanding of the tools (SC activities) and outcome measures (SFI scores) we used for particular countries.

As we discussed in Chapter Three, the SFI uses indicators of state fragility drawn from a combination of statistical databases (infant mortality, GDP per capita, coup events, leader years in office) and annual reporting (reports on political repression). Taken in the aggregate, these indicators provide a robust measure of fragility and a useful measure to help predict the likelihood of future instability, based on historical trends.[1] Taken individually, each indicator is a relatively narrow mea-

---

[1]   Marshall and Cole, 2009, pp. 21–22.

sure that does not show direct cause-and-effect relationships. The case studies describe changes in the political, security, economic, and social components of SFI but do not try to draw linkages between SC and the SFI components. Rather, they focus on the changes in each indicator to better understand the index and how levels of fragility changed in each case. For example, SC might have no impact on the security indicators of the SFI yet still improve a country's security environment, which might allow that country to provide better health care. Conversely, security indicators might improve in a country becasue of events unrelated to any SC investments. Thus, the point of the case studies is context, not causation. To summarize, the cases may help the reader better understand how and why SC investments are made and what it really means when a country's SFI score changes.

Case Study Summaries

In this section, we summarize the main findings and insights from each of the case studies, focusing on the larger patterns and on implications for the findings in our statistical analysis.

Our list of case studies consisted of the states listed in Table 5.1, in order from most SC received during 1991–2008 to least. We chose the cases on the basis of geographical diversity (based on U.S. geographic combatant commands [GCCs]), importance to the United States (as demonstrated by investments in SC), or on the basis of something unusually interesting about the specific case (e.g., the case appeared to reinforce or contradict the results of the statistical analysis, at least on the surface). In four out of five GCCs (and within the set of our 107 cases), we selected the top recipients of aid for a further look: Jordan, Georgia, the Philippines, and Colombia.[2]

Table 5.2 portrays several data points across the case studies. The assistance and SFI data come directly from the case studies and the data we developed in support of our statistical analysis. We provide

---

[2] Morocco was the top recipient in U.S. Africa Command but we chose to focus on Mali and Niger to conduct an interesting pairwise comparison.

Table 5.1
SC Recipients

Country	SC Funding ($M)	Change in SFI 1995–2008	Primary Source of SC Funding	Major Command	Key Observation
Colombia	7,591	14→12	Counternarcotics and law enforcement	SOUTHCOM	Most observers argue SC had major effect
Jordan	3,043	9→6	FMF	CENTCOM	Improved military effectiveness; advanced U.S. policies
Philippines	708	15→12	FMF Counterterrorism and counterinsurgency	PACOM	Large variation in U.S. SC policies
Georgia	337	14→9	Balanced	EUCOM	Retrain WMD scientists; stabilize restive areas; strengthen security capabilities
Yemen	131	18→16	Balanced	CENTCOM	SC effect depends on state characteristics
Honduras	110	13→8	Counternarcotics and law enforcement	SOUTHCOM	Military education a priority
Guatemala	102	20→11	Counternarcotics and law enforcement	SOUTHCOM	Professionalize military sector; improve disaster response
Azerbaijan	77	19→13	FMF	EUCOM	Improve NATO interoperability
Bangladesh	74	20→12	FMF Other train and equip	PACOM	Help professionalize military
Armenia	59	8→7	FMF	EUCOM	Improve NATO interoperability
Mali	24	20→14	Other train and equip	AFRICOM	Helped maintain security
Niger	24	20→18	Counterterrorism	AFRICOM	SC effect inconclusive

the other data points to support the case study comparisons in this chapter. For example, U.S. troop deployment data reflect U.S. forces deployed to each country during the time covered by our statistical analysis.[3] Data on partner nation defense budgets and active-duty military personnel reflect the median defense budgets and personnel levels from 2002–2008. "Education funding per troop" compares how much education-focused SC was spent on each country relative to the median size of its military (active-duty military personnel) from 2002–2008. These data and the analysis provided in each case study narrative present additional insights that complement the statistical analysis.

Comparing Case Study Data

The one observation that comes through from the case studies is that every country has its own story when it comes to SC and another story about state fragility. While there is a relationship between the two areas, its specific nature will hinge on the composition of the country SC program and the issues affecting the state's fragility. Thus, there is no "cookbook" approach to SC, but rather its application requires a careful analysis of state characteristics. Because the case study data draw from a diverse set of programs and countries over a long period, many of the comparisons provide a new perspective on how the United States is investing its SC dollars. Our key observations follow.

Substantial Variation Exists in SFI Among Most Recipients

SC levels for Colombia and Jordan were far higher than those for other countries. The Philippines received ten times more SC than Azerbaijan or Bangladesh, while Yemen received twice as much as Armenia. Guatemala received twice as much SC as Mali and Niger combined.

---

[3] Deployment data are from the Defense Manpower Data Center, which provides a quarterly snapshot of active-duty military personnel numbers by country. It does not differentiate between personnel on a U.S. military base or those conducting SC activities or other missions.

Table 5.2
SC-Relevant Information for the Case Studies

	Colombia	Jordan	Philippines	Georgia	Yemen	Honduras	Guatemala	Azerbaijan	Bangladesh	Armenia	Mali	Niger
Total SC ($M)	7,591	3,044	708	337	131	110	102	77	74	59	24	24
FMF/MAP ($M)	745	2,761	574	207	71	59	2	35	36	35	4	5
Other Train and Equip ($M)	65	241	77	104	53	9	0	25	22	12	14	12
Counternarcotics and law enforcement ($M)	6,750	1	11	9	0	24	93	8	1	5	0	2
Education ($M)	31	41	46	17	8	18	6	10	16	7	6	4
FMF as % of SC	10	91	81	61	54	54	2	45	49	59	16	21
Overall U.S. aid ($M)	8,193	7,858	3,394	2,131	638	1,565	1,601	666	2,413	1,803	1,357	441
SC as % of overall U.S. aid	93	39	21	16	21	7	6	12	3	3	2	5

Table 5.2—Continued

	Colombia	Jordan	Philippines	Georgia	Yemen	Honduras	Guatemala	Azerbaijan	Bangladesh	Armenia	Mali	Niger
U.S. troop deployment numbers[a]	1,180	470	**11,089**	165	184	9,092	310	65	189	<u>45</u>	114	135
Median defense budget ($M)[b]	**3,500**	973	909	213	823	54	158	310	785	136	120	<u>38</u>
Median size of active duty force (000s)[c]	**207**	101	106	18	67	12	29	67	126	45	7	<u>5</u>
Education funding per troop ($)[d]	<u>10</u>	35	31	94	16	**115**	18	21	<u>10</u>	22	55	34

NOTE: To highlight the greatest differences among our case studies, the highest numbers in each row (category) are in bold, and the lowest numbers are underlined. All dollar amounts are in 2005 U.S. dollars.

[a] Defense Manpower Data Center total of annual snapshots of U.S. forces deployed to each country during the time covered by our statistical analysis. DMDC data do not differentiate between personnel on a U.S. military base or those conducting SC activities or other missions.

[b] Median defense budget (millions) from International Institute for Strategic Studies, *The Military Balance*, 2002–2008.

[c] Median size of active duty force (thousands) from International Institute for Strategic Studies, 2002–2008.

[d] Median education funding (millions of 2005 U.S. dollars divided by the median size of the active duty force in millions) for 2002–2008, i.e., dollars per troop.

Military Size and Defense Budget Size, While Sometimes Relevant, Were Not the Driving Forces Behind SC Levels

Georgia received three times more SC than Yemen, although Yemen's military was about three times larger. Jordan and the Philippines had similar-sized militaries, but Jordan received four times more SC. Jordan, Philippines, Yemen, and Bangladesh had similar median defense budgets yet vastly different SC levels and activities. Georgia's median defense budget was almost one-third smaller than Azerbaijan's, but Georgia received over four times more SC.

Most Countries Had a Relatively Healthy Mix of FMF and Other SC

Although FMF/MAP accounted for over $80 billion of the SC in the data we used in our statistical analysis—twice as much as the rest of our SC programs combined—FMF made up about half of SC for half of the countries and less than that for another one-third of the countries. FMF did, however, predominate for most (but not all) countries that received the largest amounts of SC. For example, FMF made up over 90 percent of SC for Jordan. While FMF was only 2 percent of SC for Guatemala, it was 54 percent for Honduras. It was only 10 percent for Colombia—unusual for such a large SC recipient. For the Philippines and Yemen, FMF made up 81 percent of SC for the former and 54 percent for the latter.

Education-Related SC Varied Significantly, both in Absolute Terms and Relative to Military Size

Education spending totaled $46 million for the Philippines, $41 million for Jordan, and $31 million for Colombia, while all other case study countries received less than $20 million. Even among the countries that received lower amounts, there were large variations. Georgia and Bangladesh received about twice as much as Yemen and Armenia. Honduras received twice as much as Guatemala, and Mali received 50 percent more than Niger. Results are also interesting when looking at how much was spent per troop, based on median education investment and median number of active-duty personnel from 2002–2008. Education-related SC equated to about $115 per troop in Honduras but only $18 per troop in Guatemala. The Philippines received about three times more per troop than Colombia and 30 times more than Bangladesh. Yemen received less per troop than all but two other countries.

Levels of Overall U.S. Aid Also Varied Greatly, as Did SC as a Percentage of U.S. Aid

Yemen received only one-third as much aid as Armenia, one-fourth as much as Bangladesh, and an order of magnitude less than Jordan. Bangladesh received 50 percent more than Honduras or Guatemala, 78 percent more than Mali, and almost 550 percent more than Niger. While SC made up 93 percent of overall aid for Colombia, it was 39 percent for Jordan, which was the second-highest percentage, and less than 10 percent for one-half of the cases.[4]

U.S. Goals for Each Country Appeared to Be Far More Important for SC Levels and Activities Than Troop Deployments

As the case studies explain, U.S. bases in the Philippines and Honduras influenced the levels of SC provided but to very different degrees and in different ways. Other factors, e.g., counterinsurgency support in the Philippines and counternarcotics efforts in Honduras, played even greater roles shaping SC investments. The United States deployed more troops to Colombia than to any other case study country without a U.S. base, but still in numbers far lower than the relatively small U.S. base in Honduras, when aggregated over the period of this study. Jordan and Guatemala hosted the next-largest numbers of U.S. troops, but these numbers equaled fewer than 500 over the period, while all other case study countries were under 200—very small numbers for an 18-year period.

General Impressions from the Case Studies

The case studies showed that the patterns in SC levels and SFI change differed in important individual cases. Colombia, Jordan, and the Phil-

---

[4] Overall U.S. aid figures are from the USAID's Greenbook, which accounts for almost all U.S. foreign assistance, including SC.

ippines received a great deal of SC funding yet saw two- or three-point improvements in SFI, while SFI scores for relatively modest recipients, such as Mali and Bangladesh, improved by six and eight points, respectively. These differences cannot be explained by how much SC was in the form of FMF, or how much other assistance countries received, or how many U.S. troops were deployed to these countries (we did not include U.S. troop deployments in the statistical model but included them in the case studies as an additional point of comparison).

We take this as reinforcement of the observation that there are many more influences on state fragility than SC and that SFI is a useful tool for comparing countries over time, but it is less appropriate to sorting through the individual effects of these many influences. Various types of SC, other sources of assistance, partner state characteristics and actions, and exogenous factors all affect state fragility, which is captured—in the aggregate and imperfectly—through SFI scores. Large changes in a country's SFI score are the result of major changes in governance or the security environment. Our statistical analysis indicated that SC correlates with improvements in SFI scores, but SC may be just one factor among many. For example, Bangladesh shows possible linkages between SC and improvements in governance, but Bangladesh's large-scale governance improvements reflect a complex interaction of political changes, economic development, and security sector professionalization. The case studies illustrated such complexity, highlighting many of the factors that may have affected state fragility, but the degree to which SC had an impact on a particular SFI score for a particular country is impossible to assess. In no case was there a clear roadmap for success in reducing state fragility. All that can be stated is that, in the aggregate, SC is positively correlated with lower fragility.

Another observation is that how and where SC is used varies tremendously. SC is not driven simply by a handful of countries receiving billions in FMF followed by a hundred other countries receiving low levels of SC, parsed out in roughly equal shares. As the case studies show, U.S. government officials establish goals for all forms of assistance that go to partner countries and apportion different types of assistance (including SC) in support of these goals. Admittedly, the best predictor of funding levels for particular programs and countries is often the previous year's funding level, but the cases also highlight that SC levels do change substantially from year to year, with various programs growing or declining in various countries over time, sometimes dramatically. Of all the SC programs examined, IMET appeared to be the most steadily applied, which is consistent with IMET's goal of providing a low-cost, long-term investment in people and ideas. Even IMET investments, however, varied across the countries in our case studies by a factor of 10. Variations in funding also varied greatly even when taking into account the relative sizes of partner militaries.

CHAPTER SIX

Findings and Implications

Our research had the purpose of assessing the validity of a premise underlying U.S. DoD actions since 2005: that the United States can employ SC with partner states to contribute to the prevention of the rise of instability and unrest that could eventually lead to the development of terrorist sanctuaries or other adverse conditions in the states. This premise—the preventive hypothesis—has become an important aspect of U.S. global strategy and a strategic pillar for the U.S. Army.

We operationalized the research question by way of several steps. First, the preventive hypothesis was specified. Second, based on empirical linkage between states' high fragility levels and incidence of major unrest or instability, we focused on the correlation between SC and improvements in countries' fragility. The SFI served as our measure of fragility. We used data on expenditures in all the major U.S. SC programs in 1991–2008. These expenditures were then linked to all the countries where the preventive hypothesis was applicable (107 countries). We conducted statistical analyses of the relationship between SC expenditures and changes in fragility of all the states in our sample. Controls were included for every country in the analysis and for improvements in fragility over time. Furthermore, we controlled for U.S. and other countries' development aid, conflict in neighboring countries, and regime type of each recipient country. To take into account the presence of a few large recipient countries, we logged SC per 10,000 people. Periods during which the country was experiencing major political violence were removed. We assessed the impact of SC on fragility five years after the receipt of SC and conducted a variety of sensitivity analyses to ensure that our results were not artificially skewed by any one measure. In addition to our statistical analysis, we also conducted a number of case studies to gain a richer understanding of a few interesting cases. Below, we present our main findings and then move on to the recommendations that stem from our study.

Findings

We found that on average SC has a statistically significant correlation with reduction in recipient countries' fragility. The correlation for a one-year effect is strongest at the low end of expenditures per country, and there are diminishing returns from increased expenditures.

We also found that the correlation of SC was nuanced and depended on recipient country conditions. The correlation between SC and improvement in countries' fragility was stronger in countries with stronger state institutions and greater state reach. There was no statistically significant correlation between SC and changes in countries' fragility for the most fragile countries.

SC was also correlated with improvements in countries' fragility in states with more-democratic regimes. The general pattern was that, the more democratic the regime, the greater the correlation between SC and improvements in countries' fragility. In contrast, there was no correlation between SC and changes in fragility in highly autocratic regimes.

The combination of the above also meant that SC was less correlated with improvements in fragility in regions with weak state institutions, low state reach, and autocratic regimes. Conversely, SC was more highly correlated with improvements in fragility in more developed states with stronger institutions and democratic political regimes. In particular, we found a strong correlation between SC and improvements in countries' fragility in the Asia Pacific, Latin America, and Europe. We did not find a statistically significant correlation between SC and changes in countries' fragility in the Middle East or Africa.

We did not find development aid from the United States or other developed countries to have a statistically significant effect on the correlation between U.S. SC and improvements in countries' fragility. The finding mirrors some of the debates on the effectiveness of development aid and the potential longer time lag for development aid to make a difference.

Finally, we found that some types of U.S. SC are more highly correlated with reductions in fragility than others. Nonmateriel aid, such as education and law enforcement and counternarcotics aid, was especially strongly correlated. Provision of materiel aid, even though it forms most of U.S. SC, was not correlated with reducing fragility in recipient countries.

Our case studies added rich detail to the general trends we found in our statistical analyses, but the specificity of the country conditions did not allow us to come to any additional overall findings regarding U.S. SC. The case studies did show considerable fluctuations in the type of aid provided and, not surprisingly, showed strong influence from the larger priorities of U.S. defense policies.

Implications

Our research has established a statistically significant correlation between U.S. SC spending on average and improvement in the recipient country's fragility, but many unknowns still remain concerning the preventive hypothesis. Correlation was weakest in countries with high SFI scores and thus most at risk of state failure and greatest in those where instability and state failure are highly unlikely. This suggests that SC may be better at "reinforcing success" or preventing backsliding than in halting a country's decline into instability.

The finding that SC expenditures on education have the strongest correlation with improvements in countries' fragility supports the general idea that investment in human capital has large payoffs. Education is also the smallest of the categories we examined. There may be a ceiling for how effective such programs might be if they were to be more widespread.

The finding that law enforcement and counternarcotics programs appear to be more highly correlated with reduction in fragility than traditional train and equip efforts needs to be examined more closely to determine how these approaches differ. One possibility is that these programs often combine developmental and security sector aid and tend to be better integrated into broader whole-of-government efforts than traditional train and equip programs. It may also be the case that police and law and order capacity is more effective at maintaining stability than military capacity.

The lack of correlation between FMF and reduction in fragility does not mean that such aid is not useful. There are many goals for U.S. SC, and FMF may be quite effective for ensuring access, building relationships, and improving compatibility of equipment of partner militaries with U.S. forces. Better understanding of the conditions under which FMF can complement other types of SC for preventive purposes is needed.

At a more general level, our findings suggest that, in situations of high fragility, SC is not sufficient to stave off instability because highly fragile partner states may not be able to use SC effectively. This point highlights the importance of prevention (e.g., preventing states from descending to a level of fragility from which it is difficult to recover). In such cases, as well as in cases of partners lacking state reach, a more-coordinated program of development and security aid and a focus on institution building may be better. In some cases of low state reach, development assistance, with its long-term focus, may be a better tool than SC.

One of the more interesting implications of our findings concerns the concentration of effects in the early stages of U.S. SC provision. Since small amounts of SC appear to have the most return on investment and since the returns diminish rapidly, it may be that it is the fact of U.S. involvement itself—with its diplomatic and political backing—rather than its form or size that had the greatest impact on state fragility.

With judgment, the results of our study can support decision-making regarding provision of SC. Our findings suggest that there is a need for managing expectations of the effect of SC in highly fragile states. In this sense, our findings may be of interest to the GCCs that plan and deliver SC.

Finally, our findings imply that training and education efforts can help reduce fragility and prevent conflict. The increased Army focus on SC, as shown by its designating brigades for SC and aligning these units along regional lines, is a step that is in accordance with our findings, as well as with greater U.S. conflict-prevention efforts. Increased emphasis on low-footprint special operations forces efforts to build partner capacity is also in line with the preventive hypothesis that is supported by our study.

Army Security Cooperation Programs

In addition to the large-scale, DoD- and DoS-managed SC programs discussed in Chapter Three of the report, the Army (as well as the other services) manages several of its own smaller, more targeted SC programs. This appendix describes the Army programs.

The Army programs are not included in our statistical analysis because the cost is small relative to such programs as FMF or IMET. These programs are more specific than the programs in our statistical study and therefore can target key issues in the Army's SC strategy. They are also more personal, such as staff talks and foreign officer visits, and help build the groundwork of SC relationships between the United States and partner states. Managing and executing its own programs allows the Army to target specific SC needs in ways that best use Army resources. Table A.1 describes Army SC programs as of mid-2012. The programs listed here do not include those that focused exclusively on NATO or OECD countries, but several of the programs began with European partners and only recently have expanded to non-NATO Europe and other regions.[1]

There are six categories of Army SC programs:

- education and fellowships
- talks and conferences
- long-term exchanges

---

[1] These programs are Army–Army Staff Talks, Engineer and Scientist Exchange Program, Distinguished Foreign Visit, Army Global Civil-Military Emergency Preparedness, and Multilateral Interoperability Program.

- activities focused on partner state health programs
- activities aimed at increasing interoperability and sharing knowledge
- the National Guard Bureau's (NGB's) pairing of U.S. states with other militaries.

Below we discuss each of the categories of programs.

Most of the Army's programs are in the realm of training and education. That is also the realm that emerges from our statistical analysis as having the greatest impact for preventive purposes. Assuming the impact of the Army's programs is similar to the one we found for the major DoD training and education programs, we can say that the Army's programs have a strong preventive component.

Education and Fellowships

The first category of programs, education and fellowships, includes the Western Hemisphere Institute for Security Cooperation, the U.S. Military Academy (USMA) international cadet program, and fellowships at higher education institutes. Like the larger IMET program, these Army SC education programs allow international students to study at U.S. Army institutions and interact with U.S. soldiers. The institute teaches between 900 and 1,400 military, civilian, and law enforcement personnel each year and had a budget of $14 million in 2010.[2] USMA is authorized to educate up to 60 international cadets at any one time, and in 2011, 54 cadets from 31 countries were enrolled.[3] The Army Sergeants Major Academy trains up to 50 international students from some 40 countries each year, with the goal of educating enlisted soldiers for leadership in modern land warfare.[4] Last, the International

---

[2]   See the website of the Western Hemisphere Institute for Security Cooperation.

[3]   Mark R. McClellan, "USMA International Cadet Program," memorandum for the record, West Point, N.Y.: U.S. Military Academy, September 26, 2011.

[4]   U.S. Army Sergeants Major Academy, "International Military Student Office," web page, 2012.

Fellows Program at the Army War College hosts some 40 officers from 40 countries annually.[5] Foreign students bring back the knowledge they gain to their country and also forge relationships with their counterparts in the United States. The interactions stress military professionalism, as well as interoperability and effectiveness.

Talks and Conferences

The second category of Army SC programs comprises talks and conferences. Talks include the Army International Visits program, the Chief of Staff of the Army Counterpart Visit Program, Army-Army Staff Talks, and Distinguished Foreign Visitors. Visits and staff talks provide forums for small-scale interactions that introduce foreign military leaders to the U.S. Army and build personal relationships. These programs foster understanding and cooperation between U.S. personnel and foreign partners. For example, U.S. and Colombian Army staff talks in March 2012 addressed the future of U.S.-Colombian military cooperation and issues of bilateral interest, such as humanitarian and disaster response, military intelligence, and counter-IED training.[6] The Army spent about $5.3 million on Bilateral Staff Talks from 2001–2007.[7]

Conferences include the Conference of American Armies, the African Land Forces Summit, the Conference of European Armies, and the Pacific Army Chiefs Conference. The Conference of American Armies brings together commanders from 20 countries in the Caribbean and Central, North, and South America to exchange ideas and discuss mutual challenges, such as drug interdiction and peacekeeping operations. Likewise, the African Land Forces Summit brings together leaders from African countries to encourage cooperation. The Confer-

---

[5] See the website of the International Fellows Program at the U.S. Army War College.

[6] Jane Crichton, "U.S., Colombian Armies Begin Staff Talks," news article, Army.mil, March 21, 2012.

[7] Thomas S. Szayna, Adam Grissom, Jefferson P. Marquis, Thomas-Durrell Young, Brian Rosen, and Yuna Huh Wong, *U.S. Army Security Cooperation: Toward Improved Planning and Management*, Santa Monica, Calif.: RAND Corporation, MG-165-A, p. 92, 2004.

ence of European Armies has expanded since the first meeting in 1998 to include the United States, Canada, and 40 European countries. Recent topics have focused on lessons learned from multilateral operations.[8] Finally, the Pacific Army Chiefs Conference is cohosted by the United States and Singapore every two years. It brings together some 25 states from the Asia-Pacific to discuss how the land forces can help one another face contemporary challenges. Topics for the 2011 conference, for example, included, "21st century security challenges and cooperation, capabilities Asia-Pacific land forces need to have to meet these challenges, and how Asia-Pacific land forces train and develop to deter security threats."[9] These conferences allow the U.S. Army leadership to discuss the contributions that the United States can make in SC to a wide audience and help build relationships among partner states in key regions.

Long-Term Exchanges

Long-term exchanges are another category of Army SC programs. The U.S. Army Personnel Exchange Program is a one-for-one exchange program with other militaries that allows personnel from the United States and the exchanging country to operate within another military, typically for two years. The USMA International Fellows Program and Foreign Academy exchange program allow U.S. cadets to train and study abroad in 58 countries and bring international students to West Point for a one-month exchange. In addition, the Foreign Liaison Officer Program brings officers from partner states to the U.S. Army Training and Doctrine Command (TRADOC) for two to three years for information exchange.[10]

---

[8]   U.S. Army, "Conference of European Armies," *Stand To!* September 19, 2011.

[9]   Kevin Bell, "Asia Pacific Army Chiefs Participate in Regional Cooperation Conferences," news article, Army.mil, July 28, 2011.

[10]   Tatjana Christian, "TRADOC, Foreign Liaison Officers Continue to Work Together," news article, Army.mil, March 27, 2012.

Activities Focused on Partner State Health Programs

A fourth category of Army SC efforts focuses on partner state health programs. The President's Malaria Initiative and President's Emergency Plan for AIDS Relief (PEPFAR) provide humanitarian assistance to African countries and help train military and civilian partners in combating these diseases. The President's Malaria Initiative provided $1.858 billion from 2003–2011, and PEPFAR committed $46 billion from 2003–2010.[11] The U.S. Army is one of many U.S. government agencies implementing these programs. For example, Medical Command trained 342 foreign students in 634 medical courses in the United States in 2007.[12] The U.S. Army Medical Research Unit in Kenya is the only DoD infectious disease laboratory in sub-Saharan Africa, examining the effectiveness of malaria drugs and offering training in microscopy to the health community in Africa.[13]

Activities Aimed at Increasing Interoperability and Sharing Knowledge

A fifth category is the set of programs through which the Army assists partner states in increasing interoperability and sharing knowledge. For example, the Multilateral Interoperability Program helps the United States and partner states streamline command and control systems to support coalition operations and exercises. Army Global Civil-Military Emergency Preparedness (CMEP) provides education to partner states on disaster preparedness, ranging from technological to natural disasters. One CMEP program in Nepal in 2011 sought to prepare the country for a large-scale earthquake by holding the Seismic Vulnerabil-

[11] President's Malaria Initiative, "Funding," web page, 2011; The U.S. President's Emergency Fund for AIDS Relief (PEPFAR), *Using Science to Save Lives: Latest PEPFAR Funding*, undated.

[12] Department of the Army, "Information Papers: Building Partner Capacity through Security Cooperation," *2008 Army Posture Statement*, 2008.

[13] Walter Reed Army Institute of Research, "United States Army Medical Research Unit–Kenya: USAMRU-K," fact sheet, undated.

ity Procedures Workshop.[14] Security Cooperation Training Teams are managed by U.S. Army Security Assistance Command and deploy to partner states to provide advice and training on equipment and technology, as well as doctrine and tactics.[15] Army programs like these are designed to help the United States and its allies respond more quickly to global crises and threats.

The National Guard Bureau's Pairing of U.S. States with Other Militaries

NGB's State Partnership Program (SPP) pairs U.S. state National Guards with other militaries. The goal of the program is to conduct activities to enhance the defense relationship and build mutual military capability to respond to potential security threats and disasters through low-cost, tailored security engagement. Joint National Guard units and their SPP country counterparts engage in activities including small unit exchanges; military exercises; noncommissioned officer development; combat medical; homeland defense and security; disaster response and mitigation; crisis management; interagency cooperation; and border, port, and aviation security. This relationship provides the United States with strategic access, improves interoperability, and develops military capabilities for mutual security. SPP began 20 years ago (shortly after the end of the Cold War, as part of an outreach effort to the former Warsaw Pact states) and currently operates in 64 countries. The NGB FY 2011 SPP budget was $13.4 million.

Although not quantified in this study, Army SC programs contribute to the overall picture of U.S. military aid and provide benefits to both the Army and partner states. The programs discussed above are low cost relative to those included in our statistical analysis; they

---

[14] Justin Pummell, "Engineering Change in Nepal," news article, Army.mil, July 9, 2011.

[15] Security Assistance Teams are in some cases funded through FMS and IMET. See Defense Security Cooperation Agency, "Security Assistance Management Manual," Washington, D.C., undated, Chapter 11.8. See also Kim C. Gillespie, USASAC, "Security Assistance Team Trains Troops in Africa," news article, Army.mil, June 1, 2012.

are also targeted toward specific U.S. and partner state goals, such as disaster preparedness and personal relationships among military leaderships. They expose partner militaries to U.S. Army professionalism, provide education, improve interoperability, and improve partner capabilities, all of which helps integrate other militaries into regional and worldwide missions in which the United States participates.

Table A.1
Selected Army SC Programs

Title	Organization	Authority	Target Countries	Summary	Budget
Education/Fellowships					
Western Hemisphere Institute for Security Cooperation (WHINSEC)	SA	Title 10; DODD 5111.12e	Western Hemisphere	19 professional courses in the United States and 8 courses abroad taught by mobile training teams; trains 900–1,400 students each year.	U.S.$ (2010)14m
USMA International Cadet Program	USMA	Title 10	Priority countries	4-year cadetship at USMA; 60 cadets at any one time	Funded by partner states (tuition can be waived)
Sergeants Major Academy International Fellows Program	HQDA G-3/5/7, DAMO-SSR	Title 22	Priority countries	Foreign Sergeants attend Sergeants Major Academy courses; 50 seats annually; hosted 42 students from 36 countries in 2009	Grant
Command and General Staff College International Fellows Program	TRADOC/SATFA, HQDA G-3/5/7, DAMO-SSR	Title 22	Priority countries	Foreign officers attend courses at Command and General Staff College; about 124 participants annually	Grant
Command and General Staff College International Fellows Program	TRADOC/SATFA, HQDA G-3/5/7, DAMO-SSR	Title 22	Priority countries	Foreign officers attend courses at Command and General Staff College; about 124 participants annually	Grant

Table A.1—Continued

Title	Organization	Authority	Target Countries	Summary	Budget
Army War College International Fellows Program	HQDA G-3/5/7, DAMO-SSR	Title 22	Priority countries	PME program providing senior foreign officers opportunity to study, research, and write; at least 40 students from 40 countries annually	Grant; funded by partner states
Conferences/Talks					
Conference of American Armies	HQDA	Title 10	Western Hemisphere	Conferences focused on building relationships among regional militaries and discusses challenges; 20 members	Grant; funded by partner states
African Land Forces Summit	U.S. Army Africa, G-3 exercises	Title 10	Africa	Brings together land force chiefs of staff from African nations and U.S. army leadership to discuss African security challenges	Grant; funded by partner states
Pacific Army Chiefs Conference	G-35, DAMO-SSR	Title 10	Asia-Pacific	Biennial conference of land force chiefs from 25+ countries in Asia-Pacific	Grant; funded by partner states
Conference of European Armies	HQDA G-3/5/7, DAMO-SSI	Title 10	40 European nations, U.S., Canada	Land force chiefs discuss challenges, lessons learned, and interoperability	Funded by partner states
Army International Visits Program	HQDA	Arms Export Control Act (AECA)	Major non-NATO ally	Part of program that supports 6,000 official visits annually	Grant; funded by partner states

Table A.1—Continued

Title	Organization	Authority	Target Countries	Summary	Budget
Army-Army Staff Talks	HQDA G-35	Title 10	16 partner nations	Building personal and institutional relationships with partner armies; India; Indonesia; Jordan; Korea, South; Pakistan; Turkey	$5.3 million from 2001–2007
The Chief of Staff of the Army Counterpart Visit Program	HQDA, G 3/5/7, DAMO-SSIR, and DAMI-FL	Title 10	Priority countries	Visits by chiefs of foreign armies to Chief of Staff Army	SA representational funds
Distinguished Foreign Visit	HQDA G-2, DAMI-FL	Title 10	Priority countries	Visits by senior foreign officials to U.S. army counterparts, commands, and agencies	Funded by partner states
Center for Army Lessons Learned–International Engagements	TRADOC Center for Army Lessons Learned	Title 10	Priority countries	Assist partner states in creating lessons learned centers as part of Agreed to Action following staff talks or TRADOC conference	HQDA; TRADOC
Foreign Disclosure Program	HQDA-G2, DAMI-CDS	AECA	NATO; major non-NATO allies	Part of interagency program to facilitate and control sharing of classified and unclassified information with partner state governments and international organizations	Funded by partner states

Table A.1—Continued

Title	Organization	Authority	Target Countries	Summary	Budget
Foreign Exchanges					
USMA Foreign Academy Exchange Program	USMA	Title 10	30 participating nations	One-month exchange program at USMA and partner-state academies	Foreign students funded by partner states; U.S. cadets funded through grants
USMA International Fellows Program	USMA	Title 10 USMA, Language Regional Expertise and Culture (LREC) Program	Priority countries	USMA study-abroad programs; 700 cadets study and train in 58 countries	Grant from Title 10 and private donors
Foreign Liaison Officer Program	HQDA G-2	Army Regulation 380-10	Priority countries	Foreign government military and civilian employees assigned to an Army component; 20 personnel from 16 countries in 2012	Grant; funded by partner states
U.S. Army Military Personnel Exchange Program	HQDA G-35	Title 10; Section 1207; NSDD-38; DoDD 5230.20; AR614-10	Priority countries	Exchanges partner-state and U.S. Army soldiers of similar qualifications and grades under an international agreement	Funded by partner states

Table A.1—Continued

Title	Organization	Authority	Target Countries	Summary	Budget
Health Programs					
President's Malaria Initiative	MEDCOM, U.S. Army Africa	House Resolution 5501	Kenya, Tanzania	Humanitarian assistance; reduction of malaria	$1.858 billion for 2006–2011
PEPFAR	MEDCOM, U.S. Army Africa	House Resolution 5501	Kenya, Nigeria, Tanzania, Uganda, Vietnam	Humanitarian assistance; support prevention, treatment, and care programs; mil-mil and mil-civ programs	PEPFAR committed $46 billion for 2003–2010
U.S. Army Medical Department International Programs	MEDCOM	Title 22, Defense Health Program, Title 10	Major non-NATO ally	Support to GCC and Army Service Component Command Surgeon staff	Grant; funded by partner states
Multilateral Interoperability Program	Army Materiel Command	Title 10	29 countries (25 NATO)	Interoperability of command and control systems to support combined and coalition operations	Funded by partner states
Army Global Civil-Military Emergency Preparedness	HQDA G-35, DAMO-SSO	Title 10, Title 22	Priority countries	Help partner countries improve civil military disaster preparedness	Grant; funded by partner states

Table A.1—Continued

Title	Organization	Authority	Target Countries	Summary	Budget
Technical Programs					
Security Cooperation Training Teams	U.S. Army Materiel Command, U.S. Army Security Assistance Command, Security Training Management Organization	Title 22	21 countries	Teams provide advice, training, and technical support on equipment, weapons, doctrine/tactics; 41 teams of 398 total personnel in 21 countries in 2010	Funded under FMS, IMET, or generic
National Guard					
National Guard Bureau's SPP	NGB	NDAA Section 1210	63 countries	Partnerships between U.S. states and partner countries. Engaging partners via military and socio-political channels at the local, state, and national levels. Training, education, mil-mil activity	Combatant command; NGB: $13.2 million total in 2011

SOURCE: Department of the Army Pamphlet 11-31, "Army Security Cooperation Handbook," Washington, D.C.: Headquarters, Department of the Army, March 5, 2013.

NOTE: This list excludes those Army SC programs that targeted NATO and/or OECD countries.

Sensitivity Analyses

This appendix describes the sensitivity analyses undertaken for this project. All the models included in this appendix are referenced in Chapter Two.

All the sensitivity analyses are based on Model 1—"SC and SFI." The first set of analyses assesses the results' sensitivity to alternative model specifications to control for temporal dependence. The models reported in the main text are linear regressions with a lagged dependent variable, country fixed effects, and robust standard errors. Model 1a in Table B.1 replicates Model 1 in Table 4.1 using an error correction model. Error correction models use the year-over-year change in countries' fragility as the dependent variable and include both levels and changes of each of the independent variables. These models isolate the short-term (year-over-year change) and long-term (levels) effects of each of the independent variables. Model b in Table B.1 replicates Model 1 in Table 4.1 using an autoregressive model. Autoregressive models (Prais-Winston) are a two-stage process in which the temporal dependence of the overall model is estimated in the first stage and controlled for in the second. Model c in Table B.1 replicates Model 1 in Table 4.1 using a dynamic generalized method-of-moment model. Dynamic generalized method-of-moment models (Arellano-Bond) use temporal lags as instrumental variables to account for serial correlation. All three models find a statistically significant correlation between SC and improvements in countries' fragility.

Table B.2 addresses alternative constraints on the conditions in which we expect SC to affect countries' SFI scores. First, the baseline results reported in the main text exclude observations in which there was conflict in the three-year window surrounding the U.S. provision of SC; we expect that SC in these cases was more likely a response to conflict rather than an attempt to forestall conflict. Model 1d in Table B.2 includes these observations in the analysis. Second, in the baseline specification, we use a five-year lag structure to assess the impact of SC on countries' resilience. In Models 1e and 1f in Table B.2, we use a three-year and seven-year lag structure, respectively. The results from all three models are comparable to those reported in the main text.

To assess the sensitivity of our results to the inclusion of each of SFI's eight component parts, we reran our analyses excluding each dimension individually. These models are reported in Tables B.3 and B.4, as follows:

- Model SE excludes security effectiveness.
- Model SI excludes security legitimacy.
- Model PE excludes political effectiveness.
- Model PL excludes political legitimacy.
- Model EE excludes economic effectiveness.
- Model EL excludes economic legitimacy.
- Model SoE excludes social effectiveness.
- Model SoL excludes social legitimacy.

The results for each of these models are similar to those using the entire index. This suggests that no one component is driving all the results. It is important to note that this outcome is not simply the result of highly correlated components. Of the 28 bivariate correlations that exist between the eight components, all but one correlation is less than 50 percent (social effectiveness and social legitimacy correlate at 76 percent), and 64 percent of the correlations are less than 25 percent (18 of 28).

Table B.5 presents two sensitivity analyses that adopt alternative functional forms SC and for the lag structure considered for "other U.S. and OECD country international economic assistance." In the baseline analyses, we used a log linear transformation of SC to address the extreme values of SC. The results from Model 1—"SC and SFI"—

suggest that although more SC did appear to make countries more resilient, the effect of providing larger amounts of SC appeared to taper off rapidly. One concern that arises from this result is that the flatness of the relationship between SC and SFI might be an artifact of the logged scale for SFI. To address this concern, we reran the analysis in Model 1 in Table B.5 including SC squared, which is SC times SC. Including SC squared allows us to identify whether the effectiveness of SC is larger or smaller for larger or smaller amounts of SC. The results from this model—Model SC2—are almost identical to those reported in Model 1, providing further support for the relationship presented in the main text.

Second, to assess whether the mixed effects of other international assistance found in the baseline models were the result of using too short a time lag in the analysis (five years instead of the ten years hypothesized by Clemens et al., 2012) we reran the analysis including ten-year lags for official development assistance from other OECD countries and other U.S. development assistance in Model ten-year lag in Table B.5. This model provides some support for the Clemens et al. (2012) argument. Taking into account a ten-year lag, official development assistance from other OECD countries is associated with greater reduction in state fragility, and just misses statistical significance at the 90 percent level. However, the effect of U.S. assistance remains statistically not significant.

Table B.1
Sensitivity Results: Model Specification, ECM, AR1, GMM

	Model 1a	Model 1b2	Model 1c
SFI, one year prior	−0.29 *** (0.03)		0.78 *** (0.05)
SC per 10,000 people, change four years prior	−0.02 (0.01)		
SC per 10,000 people, five years prior	−0.05 *** (0.01)	−0.03 ** (0.01)	0.07 *** (0.02)
Other U.S. assistance per capita, change four years prior	0.07 (0.05)		
Other U.S. assistance per capita, five years prior	0.01 (0.05)	0.09 * (0.05)	−0.05 (0.07)

Table B.1—Continued

	Model 1a	Model 1b2	Model 1c
Development aid from non-U.S. OECD countries per capita, change four years prior	0.14 * (0.08)		
Development aid from non-U.S. OECD countries per capita, five years prior	0.17 *** (0.06)	0.21 *** (0.08)	0.10 (0.09)
Conflict in neighboring countries, year over year change	−0.11 (0.20)		
Conflict in neighboring countries	0.33 * (0.19)	0.04 (0.23)	−0.20 (0.30)
Full autocracy, year over year change	−0.01 (0.70)		
Full autocracy	0.69 * (0.39)	3.76 *** (0.60)	1.45 * (0.77)
Partial autocracy, year over year change	0.77 (0.69)		
Partial autocracy	0.92 ** (0.41)	4.56 *** (0.60)	2.03 *** (0.72)
Partial democracy, year over year change	−0.07 (0.66)		
Partial democracy	0.39 (0.34)	3.64 *** (0.55)	0.98 (0.69)
Factional democracy, year over year change	0.98 (0.68)		
Factional democracy	0.99 *** (0.37)	4.83 *** (0.58)	2.07 *** (0.73)
Constant	2.37 *** (0.43)	7.06 *** (0.14)	1.27 (0.86)
R^2	0.20	0.10	
Number of observations	1,262	1,235	1,151

SOURCE: RAND analysis.

NOTES: Standard errors in parentheses. * $p < 0.1$, ** $p < 0.05$, *** $p < 0.01$.

Table B.2
Sensitivity Results: Conflict Exclusion, Three-, Seven-Year Lags

	Model 1d		Model 1e		Model 1f	
SFI, one year prior	0.71 (0.03)	***	0.70 (0.03)	***	0.71 (0.02)	***
SC per 10,000 people, five years prior	−0.04 (0.01)	***	−0.04 (0.01)	**	0.04 (0.01)	***
Other U.S. assistance per capita, five years prior	−0.02 (0.05)		−0.07 (0.04)	*	0.02 (0.04)	
Development aid from non-U.S. OECD countries per capita, five years prior	0.14 (0.05)	***	0.10 (0.06)	*	0.06 (0.05)	
Conflict in neighboring countries	0.29 (0.18)		0.21 (0.18)		0.27 (0.18)	
Full autocracy	0.55 (0.40)		0.59 (0.35)	*	0.55 (0.38)	
Partial autocracy	0.91 (0.40)	**	0.97 (0.36)	***	0.93 (0.38)	**
Partial democracy	0.27 (0.35)		0.30 (0.30)		0.28 (0.32)	
Factional democracy	1.00 (0.38)	***	1.05 (0.33)	***	1.00 (0.35)	***
Constant	2.66 (0.43)	***	2.84 (0.43)	***	2.65 (0.42)	
R^2	0.59		0.57		0.58	
Number of observations	1,347		1,265		1,231	

SOURCE: RAND analysis.
NOTES: Standard errors in parentheses. * $p < 0.1$, ** $p < 0.05$, *** $p < 0.01$.

Table B.3
Sensitivity Results: SFI Exclusions (Models 1–4)

	Model SE		Model SL		Model PE		Model PL	
SFI, one year prior	0.68	***	0.75	***	0.64	***	0.71	***
	(0.03)		(0.02)		(0.03)		(0.03)	
SC per 10,000 people, five years prior	−0.04	***	−0.04	**	0.04	***	−0.03	***
	(0.01)		(0.01)		(0.01)		(0.01)	
Other U.S. assistance per capita, five years prior	−0.03		0.00		−0.01		−0.03	
	(0.04)		(0.04)		(0.04)		(0.04)	
Development aid from non-U.S. OECD countries per capita, five years prior	0.16	***	0.10	**	0.13	**	0.11	**
	(0.05)		(0.04)		(0.05)		(0.05)	
Conflict in neighboring countries	0.21		0.21		0.41	**	0.15	
	(0.18)		(0.15)		(0.17)		(0.17)	
Full autocracy	0.58		0.43		0.57		0.46	
	(0.39)		(0.39)		(0.38)		(0.38)	
Partial autocracy	0.98	**	0.70	*	0.86	**	0.50	
	(0.40)		(0.39)		(0.38)		(0.37)	
Partial democracy	0.30		0.27		0.30		0.29	
	(0.34)		(0.35)		(0.34)		(0.34)	
Factional democracy	1.00	***	0.87	**	1.03	***	0.39	
	(0.37)		(0.37)		(0.36)		(0.35)	
Constant	2.68	***	1.91	***	2.83		2.40	***
	(0.44)		(0.40)		(0.44)		(0.41)	
R^2	0.55		0.63		0.53		0.54	
Number of observations	1,262		1,262		1,262		1,262	

SOURCE: RAND analysis.

NOTES: Standard errors in parentheses. * $p < 0.1$, ** $p < 0.05$, *** $p < 0.01$.

Table B.4
Sensitivity Results: SFI Exclusions (Models 5–8)

	Model EE		Model EL		Model SoE		Model SoL	
SFI, one year prior	0.67	***	0.71	***	0.67	***	0.67	***
	(0.03)		(0.03)		(0.03)		(0.03)	
SC per 10,000 people, five years prior	−0.04	***	−0.05	***	0.03	***	−0.04	***
	(0.01)		(0.01)		(0.01)		(0.01)	
Other U.S. assistance per capita, five year prior	−0.02		0.00		−0.01		−0.01	
	(0.05)		(0.04)		(0.04)		(0.04)	
Development aid from non-U.S. OECD countries per capita, five years prior	0.14	***	0.14	***	0.10	*	0.07	
	(0.05)		(0.05)		(0.05)		(0.05)	
Conflict in neighboring countries	0.27		0.24		0.27		0.22	
	(0.15)		(0.17)		(0.18)		(0.17)	
Full autocracy	0.56		0.47		0.34	*	0.68	*
	(0.41)		(0.37)		(0.20)		(0.38)	
Partial autocracy	0.96	**	0.76	**	0.74	***	1.15	***
	(0.41)		(0.38)		(0.21)		(0.39)	
Partial democracy	0.24		0.23		0.06		0.34	
	(0.36)		(0.32)		(0.05)		(0.33)	
Factional democracy	1.01	***	0.95	***	0.87	***	1.10	***
	(0.39)		(0.35)		(0.14)		(0.36)	
Constant	2.15	***	2.15	***	2.75		2.58	***
	(0.44)		(0.39)		(0.29)		(0.41)	
R^2	0.55		0.61		0.55		0.55	
Number of observations	1,262		1,262		1,262		1,262	

SOURCE: RAND analysis.

NOTES: Standard errors in parentheses. * $p < 0.1$, ** $p < 0.05$, *** $p < 0.01$.

Table B.5
Sensitivity Results: SC Squared, Ten-Year Lags for OECD and Other U.S. Assistance

	Model SC2		Model 10 year lag	
SFI, one year prior	0.70	***	0.70	***
	(0.03)		(0.03)	
SC per 10,000 people, five years prior	−0.04		−0.03	***
	(0.03)		(0.01)	
SC per 10,000 people, five years prior * SC per 10,000 people, five years prior	−0.00			
	(0.00)			
Other U.S. assistance per capita, five years prior	−0.01			
	(0.05)			
Other U.S. assistance per capita, ten years prior			0.06	
			(0.04)	
Development aid from non-U.S. OECD countries per capita, five years prior	0.13	**		
	(0.05)			
Development aid from non-U.S. OECD countries per capita, ten years prior			−0.09	
			(0.05)	
Conflict in neighboring countries	0.28		0.33	*
	(0.18)		(0.19)	
Full autocracy	0.57		0.71	*
	(0.40)		(0.42)	
Partial autocracy	0.93	**	1.10	***
	(0.40)		(0.41)	
Partial democracy	0.28		0.37	
	(0.35)		(0.36)	
Factional democracy	1.01	***	1.20	***
	(0.38)		(0.38)	
Constant	2.69	***	3.08	***
	(0.44)		(0.51)	
R^2	0.58		0.59	
Number of observations	1,262		1,181	

SOURCE: RAND analysis.
NOTES: Standard errors in parentheses. * $p < 0.1$, ** $p < 0.05$, *** $p < 0.01$.

Bibliography

Army Field Manual 3-07, "Stability Operations," Washington, D.C.: Headquarters, Department of the Army, October 2008.

Army Field Manual 3-07.1, "Security Force Assistance," Washington, D.C.: Headquarters, Department of the Army, May 2009.

Army Doctrine Publication 3-0, "Unified Land Operations," Washington, D.C.: Headquarters, Department of the Army, October 2011.

Ball, Nicole, "Promoting Security Sector Reform in Fragile States," Washington, D.C.: USAID, PPC Paper No. 11, PN-ADC-778, April 2005.

Bapat, Navin A., "Transnational Terrorism, U.S. Military Aid, and the Incentive to Misrepresent," *Journal of Peace Research*, Vol. 48, No. 3, May 1, 2011, pp. 303–318.

Bell, Kevin, "Asia Pacific Army Chiefs Participate in Regional Cooperation Conferences," news article, Army.mil, July 28, 2011. As of September 18, 2013: http://www.army.mil/article/62576/ Asia_Pacific_Army_Chiefs_participate_in_regional_cooperation_conferences/

Bertelsmann Stiftung, "Transformation Index," web page, 2012. As of November 21, 2013: http://www.bti-project.org/index/

Brown, Michael E., and Richard N. Rosecrance, eds., *The Costs of Conflict: Prevention and Cure in the Global Arena*, Lanham, Md.: Rowman & Littlefield Publishers, 1999.

Burbidge, John B., Lonnie Magee, and A. Leslie Robb, "Alternative Transformations to Handle Extreme Values of the Dependent Variable," *Journal of the American Statistical Association*, Vol. 83, No. 401, March 1988, pp. 123–127.

Carleton University, "Country Indicators for Foreign Policy (CIFP)," website, undated. As of November 21, 2013: http://www4.carleton.ca/cifp/app/ffs_data_methodology.php

Center for Systemic Peace, "State Fragility Index and Matrix Time-Series Data, 1995–2012," database, Vienna, Va., 2012. As of April 1, 2012: http://www.systemicpeace.org/inscr/inscr.htm

Christian, Tatjana, "TRADOC, Foreign Liaison Officers Continue to Work Together," news article, Army.mil, March 27, 2012. As of June 11, 2013: http://www.army.mil/article/76614/

Clemens, Michael A., Steven Radelet, Rikhil R. Bhavnani, and Samuel Bazzi, "Counting Chickens When They Hatch: Timing and the Effects of Aid on Growth," *Economic Journal*, Vol. 122, No. 561, June 2012, pp. 590–617.

Collier, Paul, and Anke Hoeffler, "Unintended Consequences: Does Aid Promote Arms Races?" *Oxford Bulletin of Economics and Statistics*, Vol. 69, No. 1, 2007, pp. 1–27.

Creasey, Ellyn, Ahmed S. Rahman, and Katherine A. Smith, "Nation Building and Economic Growth," *American Economic Review*, Vol. 102, No. 3, May 2012, pp. 278–282.

Crichton, Jane, "U.S., Colombian Armies Begin Staff Talks," news article, Army. mil, March 21, 2012. As of May 29, 2013: http://www.army.mil/article/76219/

Cross, Peter, ed., *Contributing to Preventive Action*, Baden-Baden: Nomos Verlagsgesellschaft, 1998.

Defense Institute of Security Assistance Management, "The Management of Security Cooperation," Wright Patterson Air Force Base, Ohio, February 2011 and March 2013.

Defense Security Cooperation Agency, "Security Assistance Management Manual," Washington, D.C., undated. As of June 16, 2013: http://www.samm.dsca.mil/

Department of the Army, "Information Papers: Building Partner Capacity through Security Cooperation," *2008 Army Posture Statement*, 2008. As of November 20, 2013: http://www.army.mil/aps/08/information_papers/other/Building_Partnership_Capacity_through_Security_Cooperation.html

———, "Information Papers: Army Security Cooperation Support to Building Partner Capacity," *2011 Army Posture Statement*, July 2011.

Department of the Army Pamphlet 11-31, "Army Security Cooperation Handbook," Washington, D.C.: Headquarters, Department of the Army, March 5, 2013.

Department of Defense, *Quadrennial Defense Review Report*, February 6, 2006a.

———, "QDR Execution Roadmap: Building Partnership Capacity," May 22, 2006b.

———, *Military Contribution to Cooperative Security (CS) Joint Operating Concept*, Version 1.0, September 19, 2008.

———, *Quadrennial Defense Review Report*, February 2010. As of June 12, 2013: http://www.defense.gov/qdr/images/QDR_as_of_12Feb10_1000.pdf

———, *The National Military Strategy of the United States of America 2011: Redefining America's Military Leadership*, February 2011.

Department of Defense and Department of State, *Foreign Military Training*, Vol. I, joint report to Congress, fiscal years 1999–2011. As of May 29, 2013: http://www.state.gov/t/pm/rls/rpt/fmtrpt/

Department of Defense Directive 5132.03, "DoD Policy and Responsibilities Relating to Security Cooperation," October 24, 2008.

Department of State, "Congressional Budget Justification, Foreign Assistance Summary Tables," Fiscal Year 2013.

De Ree, J., and E. Nillesen, "Aiding Violence or Peace? The Impact of Foreign Aid on the Risk of Civil Conflict in Sub-Saharan Africa," *Journal of Development Economics*, Vol. 88, No. 2, 2009, pp. 301–313.

Djankov, Simeon, José Garcia Montalvo, and Marta Reynal-Querol, "The Curse of Aid," *Journal of Economic Growth*, Vol. 13, No. 3, Septembr 2008, pp. 169–194.

DoD—*See* Department of Defense.

Doucouliagos, Hristos, and Martin Paldam, *The Aid Effectiveness Literature, The Sad Result of 40 Years of Research*, working paper, Aarhus, Denmark: School of Economics and Management, University of Aarhus, 2005. As of November 13, 2013: http://ideas.repec.org/p/aah/aarhec/2005-15.html

Dube, Oeindrila, and Suresh Naidu, *Bases, Bullets and Ballots: The Effect of U.S. Military Aid on Political Conflict in Colombia*, Washington, D.C.: Center for Global Development, January 4, 2010. As of June 10, 2013: http://papers.ssrn.com/sol3/papers.cfm?abstract_id=1542699&download=yes

The Economist Intelligence Unit, "Social Unrest," web page, 2013. As of November 22, 2013: http://viewswire.eiu.com/site_info.asp?info_name=social_unrest_table

Finkel, Steven E., Aníbal Pérez-Liñán, and Mitchell A. Seligson, "The Effects of U.S. Foreign Assistance on Democracy Building, 1990–2003," *World Politics*, Vol. 59, No. 3, April 2007, pp. 404–439.

Fund for Peace and Foreign Policy, "Failed States Index," database, 2012. As of November 21, 2013: http://www.foreignpolicy.com/failed_states_index_2012_interactive

Gates, Robert M., "A Balanced Strategy: Reprogramming the Pentagon for a New Age," *Foreign Affairs*, Vol. 88, No. 1, January/February 2009, pp. 28–40.

————, "Helping Others Defend Themselves: The Future of U.S. Security Assistance," *Foreign Affairs*, Vol. 89, No. 3, May/June 2010, pp. 2–6.

Gillespie, Kim C., "Security Assistance Team Trains Troops in Africa," news article, Army.mil, June 1, 2012. As of September 17, 2013:
http://www.army.mil/article/80739/
Security_assistance_team_trains_troops_in_Africa/

Gleditsch, Kristian Skrede, and Michael Ward, "Diffusion and the International Context of Democratization," *International Organization*, Vol. 60, No. 4, October 2006, pp. 911–933.

Goldstone, Jack A., Robert H. Bates, David L. Epstein, Ted Robert Gurr, Michael B. Lustik, Monty G. Marshall, Jay Ulfelder, and Mark Woodward, "A Global Model for Forecasting Political Instability," *American Journal of Political Science*, Vol. 54, No. 1, January 2010, pp. 190–208.

Gutierrez, Francisco, Diana Buitrago, Andrea Gonzalez, and Camila Lozano, *Measuring Poor State Performance: Problems, Perspectives and Paths Ahead*, London: Crisis States Research Centre, 2011.

Hewitt, J. Joseph, Jonathan Wilkenfeld, and Ted Robert Gurr, "Peace and Conflict 2012," Boulder, Colo: Paradigm Publishers, 2012. As of November 21, 2013:
http://www.cidcm.umd.edu/pc/executive_summary/exec_sum_2012.pdf

Holterman, Helge, "Explaining the Development–Civil War Relationship," *Conflict Management and Peace Science*, Vol. 29, No. 1, 2012, pp. 56–78.

Inspectors General, Department of Defense and Department of State, *Interagency Evaluation of the Section 1206 Global Train and Equip Program*, DoD IE-2009-007, August 31, 2009.

Institute for Economics and Peace, "Global Peace Index," 2013. As of November 21, 2013:
http://economicsandpeace.org/research/iep-indices-data/global-peace-index

International Institute for Strategic Studies, *The Military Balance*, 2002–2008.

Joint Publication 1-02, *Department of Defense Dictionary of Military and Associated Terms*, August 2012.

Kelly, Terrence K., Jefferson P. Marquis, Cathryn Quantic Thurston, Jennifer D. P. Moroney, and Charlotte Lynch, *Security Cooperation Organizations in the Country Team: Options for Success*, Santa Monica, Calif.: RAND Corporation, TR-734-A, 2010. As of October 24, 2013:
http://www.rand.org/pubs/technical_reports/TR734.html

Knack, Stephen, "Does Foreign Aid Promote Democracy?" *International Studies Quarterly*, Vol. 48, No. 1, January 29, 2004, pp. 251–266.

Kosack, Stephen, "Effective Aid: How Democracy Allows Development Aid to Improve the Quality of Life," *World Development*, Vol. 31, No. 1, January 2003, pp. 1–22.

Maniruzzaman, Talukder, "Arms Transfers, Military Coups, and Military Rule in Developing States," *Journal of Conflict Resolution*, Vol. 36, No. 4, December 1, 1992, pp. 733–755.

Marshall, Monty G., *Major Episodes of Political Violence (MEPV) and Conflict Regions, 1946–2008*, Vienna, Va.: Center for Systemic Peace, 2010. As of May 28, 2013:
http://www.systemicpeace.org/inscr/MEPVcodebook2008.pdf

Marshall, Monty G., and Benjamin R. Cole, *Global Report 2009: Conflict, Governance and State Fragility*, Vienna, Va.: Center for Systemic Peace, December 2009a, pp. 21–22.

———, "State Fragility Index and Matrix 2009," Vienna, Va.: Center for Systemic Peace, 2009b. As of November 21, 2013:
http://www.systemicpeace.org/inscr/SFImatrix2009c.pdf

Marshall, Monty G., Ted Robert Gurr, and Keith Jaggers, "POLITY IV Project: Political Regime Characteristics and Transitions, 1800–2009," Dataset Users' Manual, Vienna, Va.: Center for Systemic Peace, 2009.

Mata, Javier Fabra, and Sebastian Ziaja, "User's Guide on Measuring Fragility," Oslo, Norway: United Nations Development Programme, 2009.

McClellan, Mark R., "USMA International Cadet Program," memorandum for the record, West Point, N.Y.: U.S. Military Academy, September 26, 2011. As of May 29, 2013:
http://www.usma.edu/admissions/Shared%20Documents/InterInfo.pdf

Minoiu, Camelia, and Sanjay G. Reddy, "Development Aid and Economic Growth: A Positive Long-Run Relation," *The Quarterly Review of Economics and Finance*, Vol. 50, No. 1, February 2010, pp. 27–39.

Moroney, Jennifer D. P., Joe Hogler, Lianne Kennedy-Boudali, and Stephanie Pezard, *Integrating the Full Range of Security Cooperation into Air Force Planning: An Analytic Primer*, Santa Monica, Calif.: RAND Corporation, TR-974-AF, 2011. As of October 24, 2013:
http://www.rand.org/pubs/technical_reports/TR974.html

Moroney, Jennifer D. P., Beth Grill, Joe Hogler, Lianne Kennedy-Boudali, and Christopher Paul, *How Successful Are U.S. Efforts to Build Capacity in Developing Countries? A Framework to Assess the Global Train and Equip "1206" Program*, Santa Monica, Calif.: RAND Corporation, TR-1121-OSD, 2011. As of October 24, 2013:
http://www.rand.org/pubs/technical_reports/TR1121.html

Moroney, Jennifer D. P., Joe Hogler, Jefferson P. Marquis, Christopher Paul, John E. Peters, and Beth Grill, *Developing an Assessment Framework for U.S. Air Force Building Partnerships Programs,* Santa Monica, Calif.: RAND Corporation, MG-868-AF. 2010. As of October 24, 2013:
http://www.rand.org/pubs/monographs/MG868.html

Moroney, Jennifer D. P., Aidan Kirby Winn, Jeffrey Engstrom, Joe Hogler, Thomas-Durell Young, and Michelle Spencer, *Assessing the Effectiveness of the International Counterproliferation Program,* Santa Monica, Calif.: RAND Corporation, TR-981-DTRA, 2011. As of October 24, 2013:
http://www.rand.org/pubs/technical_reports/TR981.html

Nielsen, Richard A., Michael G. Findley, Zachary S. Davis, Tara Candland, and Daniel L. Nielson, "Foreign Aid Shocks as a Cause of Violent Armed Conflict," *American Journal of Political Science,* Vol. 55, No. 2, 2011, pp. 219–232.

OECD—*See* Organisation for Economic Co-Operation and Development.

Organisation for Economic Co-Operation and Development, Development Assistance Committee data, undated. As of April 13, 2012:
http://stats.oecd.org/Index.aspx?DatasetCode=ODA_RECIP

President's Malaria Initiative, "Funding," web page, 2011. As of June 11, 2013:
http://www.pmi.gov/funding/index.html

Pummell, Justin, "Engineering Change in Nepal," news article, Army.mil, September 9, 2011. As of September 17, 2013:
http://www.army.mil/article/65252/Engineering_Change_in_Nepal/

Rajan, Raghuram G., and Arvind Subramanian, "Aid and Growth: What Does the Cross-Country Evidence Really Show?" working paper, Cambridge, Mass.: National Bureau of Economic Research, 2005. As of September 17, 2013:
http://www.nber.org/papers/w11513

Rice, Susan E., and Stewart Patrick, *Index of State Weakness in the Developing World,* Washington, D.C.: Brookings Institution, 2008. As of November 21, 2013:
http://www.brookings.edu/research/reports/2008/02/weak-states-index

Rowe, Edward Thomas, "Aid and Coups d'Etat: Aspects of the Impact of American Military Assistance Programs in the Less Developed Countries," *International Studies Quarterly,* Vol. 18, No. 2, June 1974, pp. 239–255.

Sanjian, Gregory S., "Promoting Stability or Instability? Arms Transfers and Regional Rivalries, 1950–1991," *International Studies Quarterly,* Vol. 43, No. 4, December 1999, pp. 641–670.

Savun, Burcu, and Daniel C. Tirone, "Foreign Aid, Democratization, and Civil Conflict: How Does Democracy Aid Affect Civil Conflict?" *American Journal of Political Science,* Vol. 55, No. 2, April 2011, pp. 233–246.

Serafino, Nina M., "Department of Defense "Section 1207" Security and Stabilization Assistance: Background and Congressional Concerns, FY2006–FY2010," Washington, D.C.: Congressional Research Service, RS22871, March 3, 2011.

Sislin, John, "Arms as Influence: The Determinants of Successful Influence," *Journal of Conflict Resolution,* Vol. 38, No. 4, December 1, 1994, pp. 665–689.

Szayna, Thomas S., Adam Grissom, Jefferson P. Marquis, Thomas-Durrell Young, Brian Rosen, and Yuna Huh Wong, *U.S. Army Security Cooperation: Toward Improved Planning and Management,* Santa Monica, Calif.: RAND Corporation, MG-165-A, 2004. As of October 24, 2013:
http://www.rand.org/pubs/monographs/MG165.html

USAID—*See* U.S. Agency for International Development.

U.S. Agency for International Development, *U.S. Overseas Loans and Grants: Obligations and Loan Authorizations, July 1, 1945–September 30, 2011,* Washington, D.C., 2012.

U.S. Army, "Conference of European Armies," *Stand-To!* September 19, 2011. As of November 20, 2013:
http://www.army.mil/standto/archive/issue.php?issue=2011-09-19

U.S. Army Sergeants Major Academy, "International Military Student Office," web page, 2012. As of June 16, 2013:
https://usasma.bliss.army.mil/page.asp?id=41

U.S. Army War College, "International Fellows Program at the US Army War College," webpage, undated. As of June 16, 2013:
http://www.carlisle.army.mil/usawc/dcia/external_site/ifhome/index.cfm

The U.S. President's Emergency Fund for AIDS Relief (PEPFAR), *Using Science to Save Lives: Latest PEPFAR Funding,* undated. As of April 1, 2013:
http://www.pepfar.gov/documents/organization/189671.pdf

Walter Reed Army Institute of Research, "United States Army Medical Research Unit-Kenya USAMRU-K," fact sheet, undated. As of November 20, 2013:
http://wrair-www.army.mil/documents/USAMRU-K.pdf

Weinstein, Jeremy M., John Edward Porter, and Stuart E. Eizenstat, *On the Brink: Weak States and U.S. National Security,* Washington, D.C.: Center for Global Development, 2004.

Western Hemisphere Institute for Security Cooperation, website, 2013. As of June 17, 2013:
https://www.benning.army.mil/tenant/whinsec/

White House, *National Security Strategy,* Washington, D.C., May 2010. As of November 20, 2013:
http://www.whitehouse.gov/issues/defense

The World Bank, "World Databank: Country Policy and Institutional Assessment," database, 2013. As of November 21, 2013:
http://databank.worldbank.org/Data/Views/VariableSelection/SelectVariables.aspx?source=Country%20Policy%20and%20Institutional%20Assessment

——, "Worldwide Governance Indicators," web page, 2013. As of December 11, 2013:
http://info.worldbank.org/governance/wgi/index.aspx#home

Wright, Joseph, and Matthew Winters, "The Politics of Effective Foreign Aid," *Annual Review of Political Science*, Vol. 13, 2010, pp. 61–80..